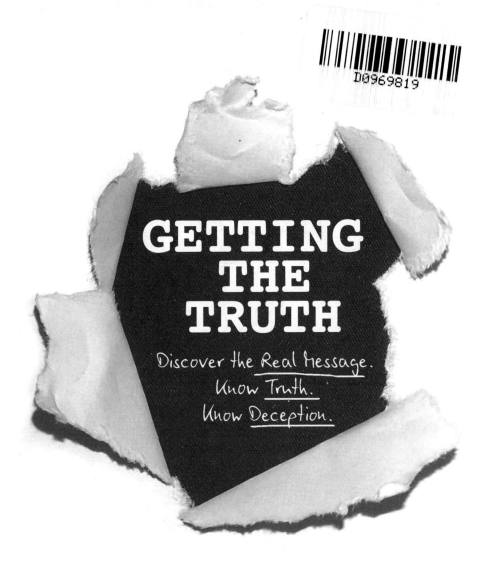

GETTING THE TRUTH

Discover the Real Message.
Know Truth.
Know Deception.

JOE KOENIG

PRINCIPIA
MEDIA

For Jackson, Ruby and Ava.

CONTENTS

MAXIMS YOU NEED TO KNOW

I provide these at the beginning so you can read them before you begin reading the main text. Remembering and understanding these maxims will greatly assist in understanding the examples and analyses. I think you'll find yourself flipping back to this page often as you go through this book. Relax. You're about to go on a great trip.

- Be an active listener — a Trained Observer.
- Always use mutually understood words in your questions.
- Be on the lookout for what is there, and more importantly, what isn't.
- We are all different, unique. Each of us communicates uniquely.
- Analysis, therefore, must be calibrated each and every time, uniquely.
- It is harder to lie, than to tell the truth.
- We experience more stress when telling a lie.
- While we promote verbosity and volume with mutually understood questions,
    The truth surfaces in simplicity and precision;
        And hides in obscurity and confusion.
- You can lose the truth in how you ask a question
    How you structure a question
        And how you position a question.

GETTING THE TRUTH

Truth-getting is more about discovering partial truths than uncovering lies. A partial truth that is misleading is a lie — let's make no mistake. But it's much easier and more productive to get the whole truth by calling a lie a partial truth. The key to truth-getting is to look through the eyes of the prevaricator, not the investigator.

Precision is the nemesis of deception. Promote verbosity and volume using mutually understood words, but look for simplicity and precision to get the truth.

The question structure determines the response. Structure your <u>initial</u> questions to promote open, uncontaminated responses. Use only mutually understood words. Look for precision, accuracy, simplicity, and directness. Then focus on where those are missing.

TRIBUTE

First of all, to the love of my life and life companion, my wife Julie. Without her love, wise counsel and support, I would have accomplished nothing.

To my kids, Katie, Jodie, Matt, and Alex; and my grandkids Jackson, Ruby, and Ava — this is for you. It's all about you.

To my late parents Kathryn and Francis, Francis and Mary Louise Vogelsang, my sisters Dawn, the late Janet Ewing, Francy O'Donnell, Barb and Kathy Vogelsang; my brothers Ferm Badgley, Bill Ewing, Mike O'Donnell, and Phil, John, Bill, and Michael Vogelsang. And to my late Grandpa Joe Koenig, an inventor and kind man, my hero and late uncle Albert Muvrin (WW II), and my late cousin Ron Jackson. All wonderful persons who positively impacted my life.

To my close friends Jack Minckler, Dick Dykehouse, Roger Bittell, Bruce Williams, the late Steve Courtney, Dr. Stuart Starkweather and my biker buddy John Van Slambrouck. And how could I forget my good buddies in the 122nd Class of the FBI National Academy.

To the mentoring and friendship of the following important people in my life: Jim Malczewski (my Senior Trooper whom I owe my love for working hard and having fun while doing it); Pat McTigue (my godfather and example-setter); Pat's wife Vivian, my high school teacher and coach Lyle McCauley, Harvey Heyer, the late Bob Robertson, the late Floyd Garrison, Sam Hutchings, Bob Nyovich, Mike Robinson, the late Dick Meloche, Phil Asiala, Bill Hassinger, Richie Davis, Frank Smith, Avinoam Sapir, John Wojnarowski, Eldon Beltz, Dan Fitzgerald, Marty Iverson, John Sadak — all mentors and teachers who helped mold my mind, my focus and my work ethic.

To Ron, Paulette, Dick, Sue, Terry, Betsy, Paul, Karen, Paul, Linda, the late Pete Panaretos, Nancy, Dean, Jack, Mary, Phil, Fay, Ricky, Marge, Maury, Phyllis, Fred, Joyce, Ade, Marge, Steve, Kathy — neighbors past and present who are all wonderful friends.

To my good friend Joel Schaaf, who introduced me to the professionals at Principia Media: Vern Jones and Dirk Wierenga, who turned my raw, obtuse product into a comprehensive and meaningful work.

I owe special thanks to Avinoam Sapir, whose work developing SCAN (Scientific Content Analysis, www.lsiscan.com/index.htm), forms the basis for much of what I explain in this book. He is the consummate teacher, as he mixes humor with challenge; subtleties with hammer blows. In short, he makes you think. He is inspirational and I recommend him to everyone.

Reid Interview and Interrogation (www.reid.com) also contributed much to my learning and grasping of the interplay between body language and statement analysis.

I owe my love and passion for getting the truth to the great organization called the Michigan State Police. If you have an interest in law enforcement, there is none better.

GETTING THE TRUTH

Like water seeking its own level, the body relieves itself of stress, seeking calmness. The greatest stress reliever known to man is truth telling. It's a relief valve, a bloodletting, a purging. Nature demands it in order to begin the rebuilding process.

What would your life be like if you knew when you were told the truth?

SYNOPSIS

This book is a digest; a compilation of over 40 years of experience, education, and research. You won't find this information anywhere else in a concise and compact book. Once you learn and master the principles provided and illustrated in this work, you will get the truth where you couldn't before — when you couldn't before. The skill and insight you will gain through this book are priceless. In short: If you master the principles in this book, you will change your life forever.

Here is what you will learn:

- Getting the truth isn't easy. The truth hides. Using my tools, you can find it.
- A complete lie is 180° from the truth. Incomplete lies, are partial truths.

- We learn at an early age to tell partial truths, to avoid telling complete lies.
- Precise communication prevents and uncovers partial truths.
- Imprecise communication nurtures deception.
- Partial truths leave tracks. It's those tracks that get you the truth.
- How to structure your questions to allow you to get the truth.
- How poorly structured questions can prohibit you from finding the truth.
- How to analyze statements to get the truth.
- Getting the truth can be very rewarding. There are great rewards awaiting you by knowing what the executive is really saying during the earnings conference; what the deposed is really saying; whether the denial is true; whether you need to do more diligence before buying, whether what your son or daughter tells you is true.

Attorneys, in particular, will find this book to be a wonderful and ready reference for preparing proper question structure for important interviews, client screenings, trials, and depositions. (See **11H**). Make sure you read this whole book, including all the statement examples and analysis of the exhibits to enable you to get the truth.

I provide analysis of many real-life examples, like the analysis on the June 13, 1994, interview of O.J. Simpson by Los Angeles Detectives Tom Lange and Phillip Vannatter — the day after the murders of Nicole Simpson and Ronald Goldman (a portion from Exercise 13A) :

Vannatter: Yeah. When was the last time you saw Nicole?

"Last" is an excellent word and "the last" requires a precise response. There is only one "last" time. How would the killer answer this? It's a live torpedo in the water.

This is a critical question, and it's asked halfway into the interview. As part of our interview/deposition/trial strategy we must construct our critical questions and place them in the interview at strategic locations. I like the location of this critical question. It allows for calibration (see Chapter 3). Preliminary questions set the stage for well- founded analysis of responses to critical questions.

Critical questions must be structured simply, precisely, and carefully. I would have liked this critical question to read, "When did you last see Nicole?" That question uses fewer words (6 instead of 8) and is slimmer, sharper, and more compact. It carries more of a punch, like a shaped explosive. These questions have to be clear, concise, sharp, and cutting in order to separate the innocent from the guilty, the deceivers from the truth-tellers. The cutline between the two often requires the precision of a diamond cutter. The more time spent on the structure of critical questions, the better.

Simpson: We were leaving a dance recital. She took off and I was talking to her parents.

There was no discussion about what happened the night before (the night of the killings) up to this point. This is the beginning of Lange and Vannatter's attempt to reconstruct where O.J. was the night before. This is a very critical question. O.J. responds to this very specific time request with, "We were leaving," which is not time specific. A response of, "We left," would be much more responsive. Also note that Vannatter asked for "the last time," not, "the last place." Instead of a time, O.J. responds with, "a dance recital," which isn't a time. It's not even an approximation of a time. A response like "the dance recital," or "we left a dance recital last night," would have been much more responsive, but still not sufficient. With the response, "We were leaving a dance recital," O.J. is being non-specific, general, and imprecise. His answer is not definitive or finite. It's not a clear, simple, or precise response.

Remember, O.J. is being questioned about murdering two people. He knows he's a suspect in those murders. This question is critical in determining when he "last saw" Nicole. If you were asked this question and you didn't commit the homicides, you would make sure you provided a specific, precise answer, saying, "7:30 PM," or "When we left the dance recital last night." You would want to prove your innocence. You wouldn't be imprecise and careless and say, "We were leaving a dance recital." He substitutes an "a" for "the" and it provides O.J. with the ambiguity and intentional obfuscation necessary to avoid telling a complete lie. If he were the killer, to say, "When we left the dance recital," would be a complete lie. (A liar's reluctance to tell a complete lie and preferred use of partial truths to deceive is explored in Chapter 2). A truth teller would use "the" not an "a." Deception is designed to be subtle, almost imperceptible. This is deception.

Also, the "took" in "She took off" suggests a lot of emotion. He could have said, "She went" or "She left" but O.J. chose "took." This suggests anger and/or emotion before she departed. The words "left," or, "went," reflect much less emotion. Also, "talking to her parents" is not a direct response to the question, it is a deflection. Pay particular attention to deflections. They are evidence of sensitivity to the question and an attempt to fill the time and take the interview off track. I like the question and the timing of it. I would like a better-worded critical question. And they needed to force O.J. to respond with clarity and precision to get the truth.

Through the above analysis you can discern so much more. That's why this book is entitled, "Getting the Truth." I could have titled it "Learning the Truth," or "Knowing the Truth," or "Understanding the Truth." But those words are too passive to get the truth. You need to be diligent, passionate, aggressive, understanding, and empathetic to get the truth. The word, "Getting," tells you that the truth isn't something that just surfaces. You need to go after it, find it, sense it, and finally understand it.

This is also about becoming a Trained Observer and gaining a better understanding of what you are told and what you read. And what you aren't told and what you don't read. What you are told is very important. What you aren't told may be even more important. Whether you're a parent, an investor, an attorney, a businesswoman, a consultant, an analyst, or an investigator — you will become better at making decisions if you truly understand what is going on around you. We are flooded with communications of all forms. Knowing the true meaning of all those messages and non-messages will make our lives easier, more profitable, more efficient, and less confusing. It's all there. We just have to learn how to absorb it. To know why we didn't see it or why we didn't hear it. It's all there, even when it appears it isn't. If they didn't answer it, they did. If they didn't deny it, they did it. The absence of evidence is not evidence of absence. Come along. Let's go on this journey together.

GETTING THE TRUTH

Truth-getting is more about discovering partial truths than uncovering lies. A partial truth that is misleading is a lie — let's make no mistake. But it's much easier and more productive to get the whole truth by calling a lie a partial truth. The key to truth-getting is to look through the eyes of the prevaricator, not the investigator.

"You callin' me a liar?" yelled the young gunslinger, menacingly, while adjusting his weapon.

"No, sir. You told the truth, just not completely," I said.

"Oh. OK."

THE COST OF LYING

What do lies cost us? Or, as you will learn, what do partial truths (deceptions) cost us? The answer is simple: gazillions!! And the cost, unfortunately, is not just in dollars.

"Everybody has an agenda; And everybody is lying to you."
—John Ficarra, Editor Mad Magazine
10/29/2013 CNN

Nothing turns a jury against you faster than when they learn you lied to them. Does anyone lie to his or her physician? What price did the victims of Bernie Madoff pay? What price did President Clinton pay — or his family? What price do parents pay when they are deceptive to their children? What price did we Americans pay for the 2009 mortgage and financial crisis? What is the cost when an executive of a publically traded company tells us the books are rosy when, in fact, they're not? What is the cost when our child leads us to believe he is not on drugs when he is? Or, when we intentionally deprive ourselves of the truth, by not doing something, or not finding something — when we could have, when we should have?

Deception is all around us. It permeates our everyday lives and it is destructive — financially, emotionally, and physiologically. I'm tired of it. And you should be too.

This book is about trying to add some light to this world. Cast some light on how to identify partial lies (deception). Be able to see in the shadows and dark spots. It will help you know when you're being told the truth. Help you discern between truth, partial truths, and fiction. Assist you in making better factual decisions. See what lies underneath. See what can't be seen. Realize that even nothing takes up space.

She asked the Sheriff: "Was that a true story?"

Sheriff (Tommy Lee Jones) "Well, I can't swear to every detail, but it is true that it was a story."

—The 2007 Movie - <u>No Country for Old Men</u>

Chapter 1

BECOMING A TRAINED OBSERVER

A Trained Observer is one who simulates Mother Nature, every hour, and every day. She senses everything that occurs and doesn't occur all around her. Her reactions

"Two-thirds of the forest's ecosystem is underground."

—Nature TV 4/2013

are fact-based — and she never makes a mistake. Nothing happens without a reason. For every action, there is a reaction.

A Trained Observer uses finely tuned skills, tools, and all senses: seeing, hearing, tasting, touching, and smelling.

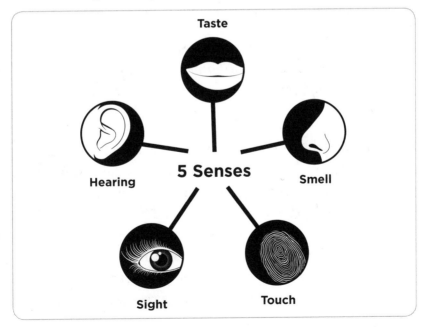

To become Trained Observers we need to train ourselves to see without filters, to hear without distinguishing, to taste without discriminating, to touch without reacting, and to smell without concluding. Simply put, we need to be objective. Know and identify your prejudices and work hard to set them aside.

And there should be a sixth sense — one that kind of parallels the other five. One that should always be there, in full use, and operational: empathy. Without empathy, you will not become a Trained Observer. Empathy isn't feeling sorry for someone — that's sympathy. Sympathy causes a bias that will keep you from getting the truth. Empathy is much more neutral than sympathy. Empathy is putting yourself in their shoes, using all your senses to experience what they experience. That requires research, patience, work, and commitment. Empathy is a means to understand. It's only through the peephole of understanding that you can "see" the true message.

So, how do we get there?

Empathy embraces the following:

"We are for difference: for respecting difference,
for allowing difference, for encouraging difference,
until difference no longer makes a difference."
—*Johnnetta B. Cole*

So, OK, most of us don't live up to that lofty standard. We should, but we're human. But, the point is made. Your biases, opinions, judgments, even sympathy, will all interfere with your reception system. We need to minimize (eliminate?) those. A much less productive option is at least to know your biases, opinions, and judgments so you can work around them. Simply put: If you judge, before you absorb — you won't receive the true message. If, by chance, you receive it, you still won't understand it.

So, to be Trained Observers, to be good at discovering the truth, first look inward. Fix the receiver first. Then receive. That requires a great deal of work and sometimes courage. Some are naturals. Some, like me, have to work very hard at it. We can all become better at it. Kids are excellent receivers.

So, let's assume the receiver is OK. Onward we go.

Let's pause and absorb the powerful and penetrating lyrics of Simon and Garfunkel's, *The Sounds of Silence (the first two lines)*:

> *Hello darkness, my old friend*
> *I've come to talk with you again*

The beauty of that song and the words tell us what we need to know. We need to listen. We need to communicate. We need to feel empathy. We need to see, hear, taste, touch, and smell what's going on around us.

- The veteran police officer sees suspicious activities that other mortals miss.
- The experienced carpet cleaner sees carpet stains that I never could.
- The medical doctor sees and feels to help determine what's wrong with our bodies.
- The psychiatrist listens and carefully asks well-structured questions to reveal our dark, destructive thoughts and memories to help fix our minds.
- Our dogs can distinguish sounds and smells in ways that amaze us.
- We have tools that search without moving anything, without disturbing anything to allow us to see what we can't see on the surface.

And it goes on and on. We can train ourselves to become better at discovering the truth. I always make a mental note to turn on my "Trained Observer" switch. So, make it a conscious act to be sure your "Trained Observer" switch is in the "On" position. It takes training, time, patience, and practice.

Astronomers use Averted Vision (using peripheral vision to "see" a planet or star). They see an object, especially a moving object, by not looking at it!

Boxers learned long ago that they could react to a moving object (a punch) much quicker using their peripheral vision than their direct vision. They could avoid punches instead of absorbing them. I learned this brutal truth while in Michigan State Police Recruit School boxing classes.

The American Indian always strived to be feeling at one with everything, that each person is a part of everything and everything is a part of each person. In that way, the American Indian approach what Johnetta B. Cole was striving for — "... until difference no longer makes a difference." Much can be learned from the American Indian.

It was the old Inuit who helped teach the scientist (Tyler Smith) in the movie, "Never Cry Wolf," the real secret to create a thriving caribou herd. The Inuit lore helped the scientist to see what he wouldn't have seen had it not been for the old, learned Inuit. The scientist learned the wolf helped keep the herds healthy by killing the sick, lame, and elderly caribou, allowing the remaining caribou to thrive on the limited food supply. Again, another lesson from Mother Nature delivered by the old Inuit. And, I must quote the Inuit song used at the end of the movie to help put everything into perspective:

"I think over again my small adventures, my fears.
Those small ones that seemed so big.
For all the vital things I had to get and to reach.
And yet there is only one great thing, the only thing:

*To live to see the great day that dawns
and the light that fills the world."*

AND SO IT GOES . . .

If you focus on one thing, you'll miss another. Had the scientist not met the old Inuit, had he not been open to the teachings of the old Inuit, he wouldn't have "seen." As we focus, we lose our ability to absorb all the information. Stay open. The longer we stay in receiver mode, the better.

The key to becoming a Trained Observer is to unfocus, to use our senses in a peripheral way, to absorb without recognition. Then the interpretation process begins, but not before absorption begins to end. The recognition process begins just before the interpretation process. Force yourself to absorb, delay recognition, recognize what you absorbed following the absorption — then interpret what you absorbed.

Absorption

Begin Recognition

Interpretation/Analysis

If you begin interpretation before you've absorbed all the information, you cannot interpret all the information. If you reach a conclusion based on insufficient information, you will prejudice yourself against reaching the correct decision. If you begin to recognize the information before you absorb all of it, you will miss information. It is a linear process that must be followed. One cannot start until the other finishes. Again, apply training, patience, and practice.

That's what I strive to follow. I must say I don't always "absorb" as long or as much as I should. You can't always follow it. We all have time pressures to gather the facts and reach correct conclusions. The above model is how it should be done. It's a goal — always try to achieve it.

Turn your internal rheostat to Full Absorption. Know all that is going on around you.

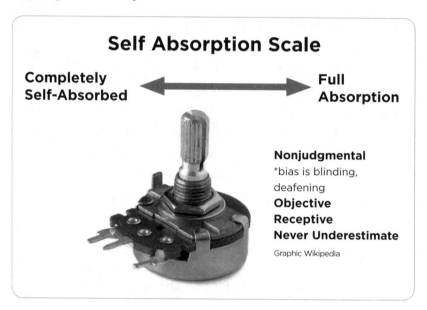

Self Absorption Scale

Completely Self-Absorbed ⟵⟶ Full Absorption

Nonjudgmental
*bias is blinding, deafening
Objective
Receptive
Never Underestimate

Graphic Wikipedia

THE OLD CHEROKEE GOT IT RIGHT

An elder Cherokee Native American was teaching his grandchildren life lessons. He said to them, "A fight is going on inside me. It is a fight and it's between two wolves.

One wolf represents fear, anger, envy, sorrow, regret, greed, arrogance, self-pity, guilt, resentment, inferiority, lies, false pride, superiority, and ego.

The other stands for joy, peace, love, hope, sharing, serenity, humility, kindness, benevolence, friendship, empathy, generosity, truth, compassion, and faith.

The same fight is going on inside you and inside every other person too."

They thought about it for a minute and then one child asked his grandfather,

"Which wolf will win?"

The old Cherokee replied, "The one you feed."

One will get the truth. The other won't.

And, again, another example from one of President Clinton's quotes:

"I want to say one thing to the American People. I want you to listen to me. I'm going to say this again. I did not have sexual relations with that woman, Ms. Lewinski."

—President Clinton.

You will learn later in this book to look at the introductions to statements. Here, President Clinton uses, "I'm going to say this again. . ." You will learn why you can't rely on statements that follow an introduction like this. Remember, it doesn't mean the statement is not true, only that you cannot rely on it.

Throughout this book, I'll provide quotes, excerpts, and exercises to help illustrate my points. Getting the truth is very challenging. I sometimes ruminate for hours over the subtlety of a word or phrase the subject used in order to determine the true message. Truth-getting takes a lot of work and practice.

Chapter 2

WHEN IS A LIE, A LIE?

Webster's definition of the verb, "lie," is "to create a false or misleading impression," "to make an untrue statement with intent to deceive."

So, the key words to define a lie are:

1. "untrue statement with intent to deceive,"
2. "to create a false or misleading impression,"

Sounds ominous, doesn't it? Remember the song written by Billy Mayhew (the first two lines)?

"Be sure it's true when you say, 'I love you' It's a sin to tell a lie.
Millions of hearts have been broken Just because these words were spoken..."

So, it's part of growing up. A lie is a sin. A lie is bad. How many others have said, "Don't you lie to your mother!" Why is there so much emphasis on lying? And when do we learn to lie? And why?

"Child-development experts used to be unsure if young children were capable of telling a lie. Sure, they could pretend, joke around, report things incorrectly. But deliberately attempt to deceive another person? Now

they know what many parents already suspected: All kids do it. Victoria Talwar, Ph.D., a leading researcher on the subject at *McGill University*, in Montreal, says that the act of manipulating the truth for personal gain "is a developmental milestone, much like learning to get dressed by yourself or to take turns." Indeed, studies show that bright kids (who are capable of making up a story and getting others to believe it) can pick up the skill as early as age 2 or 3. And their peers catch up quickly: By age 4, Dr. Talwar says, it's game on — all children stretch the truth at times."
—Sharlene K. Johnson, Parent Magazine, July 2013.

THE AXE STORY

I grew up in a small Midwest community. I was always inquisitive, flipping rocks to see what was under them; capturing salamanders, worms, snakes, butterflies. Days were filled with baseball, fun, and ice cream. Life was good. But all of that had a price.

At the age of 4, I was everywhere. I broke front windows with snowballs and stones, having to sell seeds to pay for their replacements. I was known to have the best arm and aim in the neighborhood and, like a gunslinger, proved it many times. I suffered a hundred bee stings when, on a challenge, I threw a stone and hit a beehive from 20 yards away. My buddy who prompted me to throw it, stood like a rock while I foolishly ran at what I thought was light speed. All the bees hit the moving target. They missed the schemer behind it all only because he didn't move. Like the little boy who stood silent while his brother admitted to their mother that he took a cookie escaped punishment because he didn't say anything.

It was 1950. My neighbors up the hill from my house, the Tuiniers, just installed a cement driveway. In those days, cement driveways were two strips of concrete. The still-curing concrete had sharp, jagged edges exposed by the ditches dug for the freshly removed wooden frames.

The Duttons lived on the other side of my house. Mr. Dutton had a detached garage that stood alone at the base of a hill. In those days, most garages were detached. I loved going into that garage, exploring, and playing with his tools. It was quiet, like a tree house in that it was sitting there all alone, always full of new tools and projects. I wasn't supposed to be there, and I knew it. I was in there all too often. Mr. Dutton told my mom in no uncertain terms to "keep that kid out of my garage."

One day I was playing on Mr. Tuinier's new driveway, slipped, and scratched the top of my left knee. It drew a trickle of blood. Bored, I headed to Mr. Dutton's garage.

I always liked opening the door to see what was new. I turned on the light and always stood there for few seconds, looking for anything new. Mr. Dutton was always doing something in there, always a new project. On this day, he had an axe on his tool table — illuminated like a flower in a ray of sunlight. On the garage floor was a tree stump. I picked up the axe, or tried to. It was so heavy I had to brace myself and pick it up with both hands. I was dead set on swinging it at the stump. I swung, missed the stump, and embedded the blade just below my left knee.

Wow! Blood all over. The cut was vertical, long and deep. I ran crying to my mom in the house. She gasped, then blurted, "Joey — What happened!!!?" I responded, with a slight, almost imperceptible pause . . . "I fell on Mr. Tuinier's driveway!"

Well, that's the beginning. I was no different than anyone else. We learn at an early age to tell partial truths. We learn there are "White Lies." A white lie is defined by Dictionary.com as "minor, polite, or harmless lie; fib." So there are different kinds of lies. We call them fibs, half-truths, whoppers, tall stories, etc. We rationalize it's not a real lie when there is some truth to it. And we excuse ourselves. It's OK. There is some truth to my statement, "I fell on Mr. Tuinier's driveway." I did fall on the driveway, but I knew my mom wasn't focused on the tiny scratch that resulted from the driveway fall. She (and I) was staring at the gaping wound from the axe! But it worked.

I told a partial truth to avoid punishment. But there was enough truth, a modicum, which was sufficient for me to safely convince myself I told the truth. I knew there were consequences if I admitted it happened in Mr. Dutton's garage. We may tell partial truths to further our agendas. We may do it to keep pain from someone we love. We may, as in my case, do it to avoid receiving pain. There are many reasons and excuses. So, when is a lie, a lie?

A lie is a lie when we say, "I did not do it," when I did it, and everyone knows what "it" is. It is a statement that is 180° from the truth — when it is diametrically opposed to the truth. Anything short of saying "I didn't do it" when I did it is not a real lie. If the statement has some modicum of truth in it, we believe it's not a real lie. So when I said, "I fell on Mr. Tuinier's driveway," I told a partial truth — and therefore not a lie. A partial truth is not a lie. We've convinced ourselves that partial truths are not lies. Real lies are extremely rare. I don't think they exist. They're kind of like dark energy. Although now we think they've discovered that!

Think of a complete lie as infinity. We approach it, but we never quite get there. And, as you'll later learn, it's only a complete lie if it stands on its own. And is 180° from the truth. If, for example, I were to say, "I can say I didn't do it," — that's not a complete lie. Because of the introduction (Chapter 6), that isn't a lie. "I can say. . ." allows me to say it and I did say it — so, it's a partial truth.

The good part for investigators/analysts/professionals/parents/investors is that partial truths leave tracks. This book is about discovering those tracks. That's how they discovered dark energy too. Dark energy leaves tracks.

> "She was not choked. She was not punched."
>
> —Pastor Dollar 6/10/12

Well, Pastor Dollar, you could have said "I did not choke her. I did not punch her." That would have shown more commitment and truthfulness. The fact you didn't makes this statement less credible.

Chapter 3

TRACKS

When I arrived home, bloodied, crying, and all out of sorts, I left an obvious track (trail of blood) from Mr. Dutton's garage to my back door (although to my benefit, you can't see blood very well in grass). But I left another, just as important track. The track I left when I told my mom, "I fell on Mr. Tuinier's driveway," was that slight, almost imperceptible pause between the question and the answer. If I had video of that moment, we would see me looking like a deer in headlights gasping and groping for a way out. Mom had me cornered, I was bleeding and out of control, but I mustered enough moxie to blurt out the best thing I could come up with — and I succeeded! It was at that moment (or close to it) when I learned that telling a partial truth can be a win-win.

I guess I sort of knew at an early age that I would become a wordsmith,

When wolves and dogs reach the crest of a hill, they always slow down and stop. They stop to look for what's ahead, and what's below.

Simplicity is the key to getting the truth. The truthful and complete statement or response is simple, clear, precise, and direct. Anything else is suspicious.

a linguistic analyst, at some point in my life. While I always did well on tests, I was a slow reader.

As I read, I'd get distracted on some word or phrase or thought. The phrase I recently wrote on Facebook is a good example: "Happy Birthday to my lovely life-long love of my life, my wife, Julie!!" While trying to read that, I would take several minutes just to experience the difficulties of saying it! So, I'd enjoy the nuances, rhythm, and physicality of the pronunciation process. How about this old and famous locomotive cheer for Kalamazoo Central High School?

> *K-A Ka L-A La M-A Kazoo*
> *Kalamazoo Zip Zam*
> *Celery City of Mich-i-gan*
> *Kalamazoo Rah! Kalamazoo Rah!*

Then I'd get so caught up in that, that I had to reread the passage to understand or comprehend it. So, while I love to read, it was a chore. What helped me was a reading course called Evelyn Wood, which taught me how to overcome those seemingly non-productive tendencies. As it turns out, those tendencies make me the linguistic analyst I am today.

So, we leave "tracks," when we tell partial truths. The first few seconds of a response are very important to a truth detector. For example, in my response to my mom, the pause was a giveaway that I was creating a response. There should be no hesitation when telling your mom what happened when your leg has a deep gash in it! The cause is something you don't forget! Likewise, when people are asked a question, the response should flow in accordance with their linguistic habits.

Tracks take on different shapes and forms. The blinking of the eye(s), curling of the lips, lip biting, breathing patterns, pauses, and many other facial and body expressions that are or are not in sync with what the person is saying and thinking are all important.

The blinking of eyes is very important. Many people will blink when they make an important point, or end their thought process. A blink that is out of context is a window into what the person might be thinking. The pattern established in the opening session where nonthreatening questions are asked will help identify when there is an out of the ordinary blink when threatening questions are asked. An out of the ordinary blink is what you're looking for and, together with other clues, will help you obtain truthful information.

The rate of eye blinking may tell you much about whether a person is lying and may even tell you immediately after they've told a lie. In a study entitled, "Blinking During and After Lying," conducted by Sharon Leal and Albert Virj (Springer Science & Business Media, LLC 2008), the finding was that eyes blink less when people are lying than when they're telling the truth. The theory is that it takes more cognitive demand to tell a lie than to tell the truth when "people are motivated to be believed." The study showed that truth tellers blinked more frequently than liars when the critical statements were made. My experience only corroborates those findings. Eye blinking is an important tool in getting the truth.

The curling of the lips is often a clue into whether the person is confident in what they are telling you. A person telling the truth will not end his/her truthful comment with the lips curled down. The one telling the partial truth will curl their lips down.

When someone is recounting a past incident, the first thing we expect in a truthful response is a simple, clear, precise, and direct statement. Further, we look for first person singular pronouns specifically, personal pronouns, past tense verbs, all in the active voice. The active voice is a statement where the actor commits the act. It shows commitment by the actor. "I threw the ball," is the active voice. There is no doubt who threw the ball.

Contrarily, "The ball was thrown and the glass was broken," is the passive voice because we don't know the actor. Who threw the ball? The passive voice allows no commitment. Look closely at the passive voice in statements. You will find many deceptive statements in the passive voice, especially if the subject shows he/she can speak in the active voice. See **11A**.

The analyst has to calibrate to the person being analyzed. In addition to what I've detailed above, take note of the person's pitch, rhythm, prosody, elisions, contractions, melody, sentence length, vocabulary, eye movements, body movements, eyebrow movements, twitches, thought development, head movements, inconsistencies of any kind, etc. All of these can be calibrated as the standard during the introductory phase where the discussion is nonthreatening, informal, casual. Then gauge that calibrated standard to the behavior during more formal discussion or questions. But you need to be careful, because you may be engaging in threatening discussion while you are in the "nonthreatening, informal, casual" phase. I had a case where I asked the question, "Where do you live?" which I thought was of the nonthreatening, informal, casual category when it, in fact, was the question that broke my case. The subject had difficulty answering this seemingly innocuous question. The subject was in charge of vendor contracts for the organization. I discovered he was living free in a vendor provided apartment. The subject subsequently lost his job. So, you have to be aware and careful at all times.

It may take many years to become confident in relying on these observations, but once you've mastered it, the analysis will be very illuminating. It's the inconsistencies in each of these that leave the tracks that truth-getters see. How does the subjects' response to stress questions differ from their responses to non-stress questions? The tracks left by these inconsistencies are what reveal the truth.

"I have never sexually harassed anyone, let's say that."
— Presidential candidate, Herman Cain
10/31/2011 on Fox News.

The qualifier, the retroactive introduction, "let's say that," makes the statement unreliable. Even though the introduction was inserted after the statement, it nevertheless, makes what came before it unreliable. (See Chapter 6 on Introductions) Also, Mr. Cain could have been specific and named the woman (women) accuser(s). A more believable denial would have been, "I didn't sexually harass Ms. Xxxxx." The fact that he chose not to make his denial in this form makes his denial less credible. Remember, the simpler the denial, the better. The more direct the denial, the better.

Chapter 4

ALVIN —
THE COMMUNICATION PROCESS

For simplicity's sake, we will call the human communication process "**Alvin**." Each of us has our own unique way of communicating, but we do have a standard communication model. Below is a graphical representation of Alvin (formally known as the Claude

"I always say what I mean. And I always mean what I say."
—Vice President Joe Biden
10/11/12.

Shannon and Warren Weaver Communication Model, 1947).

Alvin (Communication Process)

Channel

Source (Sender)-->Encoder---*Noise*----->Decoder-->Receiver

Message

Feedback

Let's use a typical interview setting (one interviewer and one subject being interviewed, the receiver) to help simplify and explain Alvin. First the interviewer (Source or Sender) thinks the thought. The thought is then converted (Encoded) to the English Language words from the sender's vocabulary. The mechanism for selecting those words is similar to what a parking valet does when you ask for your car. You hand the valet your receipt, which shows where your car is parked and the valet retrieves your car. Our word selection mechanism works much the same way. Our brain tells the mechanism to select the exact word/phrase we need to send the message we want to send, the way we want to send it. This is a careful and precise process. The words are then transmitted by the sender's mouth (Channel) through the air (Channel & Noise) to the receiver's Decoder (Ears). The receiver, who speaks the same English Language, hears, decodes, and eventually (hopefully) understands the words expressed by the sender (interviewer). The receiver also has a little internal parking valet (mechanism) as well which uses the receiver's unique vocabulary and the receiver's unique definitions to interpret the sender's message. This understanding between the two is perceived through Feedback. This is all done at varying speeds but close to the speed of light. It's no wonder we have trouble communicating. And, it's no wonder that people can hide the truth in their messages.

Remember, this process isn't pure and it has all kinds of obstacles and barriers. There is noise throughout. The interviewer's nasal voice (noise) may interfere with the receiver's thought process because of the receiver's bias against nasal sounding voices. Is the sender contaminating the response through the use of improperly structured questions? The room could be too warm or cold. There could be real noise from outside the interview room that interferes with the hearing of the receiver. The sender might be irritated from something someone said to him just before the interview and the visible irritation confuses the receiver. The receiver may have just learned of his father's death (unfortunate noise). There could be many, many sources for noise in this process. Suffice it to say: Communication is complex and very difficult.

The sender and the receiver each have their own unique Alvin. Based on their individual vocabularies, physical and chemical peculiarities, interpretations, thought processes, training, abilities, biases, prejudices, past experiences — each may interpret the intended message differently, uniquely.

To understand further, let's look at a written or oral response prepared by the receiver in response to a sender's question. The writer's choice of words, the way they're used, the words' positions in the sentence, the writer's body language used as the word is written or said, her eyes, facial expressions, lips, eyebrows, inflections, rhythm, rhyme, whether the words she used were contractions, whether the words used are expected or unexpected, and so on. Look for harmony and disharmony. Communication is music; and music is communication. All of that is the communication process. We can never achieve perfect communication. But we can approach it. We approach perfect communication by:

> *Knowing what is said and why;*
> *And, knowing what isn't said*
> <u>*and*</u> *why it isn't said.*

There is even communication when nothing is said. Nothing can be communication. Remember, nothing takes up space. One day, I was about to interview an employee regarding a suspected embezzlement. As we entered the interview room, before a word was said, before anything was done, she let out a small, almost imperceptible sigh. Remember, like water seeking its own level, the body relieves itself of stress, seeking calmness. She wanted to confess to relieve her stress. Later, she did. And I knew she would before she said a word.

Empty is Useful

Thirty spokes unite at the single hub;
It is the empty space which makes the wheel useful.

Mold clay to form a bowl;
It is the empty space which makes the bowl useful.

Cut out windows and doors;
It is the empty space which makes the room useful.

When there is something, it is beneficial;
When empty, it is useful.
—Lao Zi, Chinese Poet/Philosopher

What you see is beneficial. What you don't see is useful.

"Obama and Merkel spoke by phone earlier Wednesday and 'the president assured the chancellor that the United States is not monitoring and will not monitor the communications of the chancellor,' White House press secretary Jay Carney said."
—Politico 10/23/2013

More often than not, it's what isn't said that is important. We need to tune in to our subjects, calibrate to them. See what isn't there. What isn't there will often tell us what happened or what the message really means. In the above quote, the missing information tells the story. Jay Carney never said anything about past monitoring.

So, to really communicate and to understand, we need to know what was said, what wasn't said, and why. Two close friends can communicate almost perfectly by not saying a word. Longtime partners rely on what they hear, what they don't hear, the sighs, the breathing patterns, the pauses, to gain a better understanding of what their partner really means. And sometimes we just don't listen as we should. Look at this example:

"Dear Abby,
I've suspected that my husband has been fooling around but when confronted with the evidence, he denied everything and said it would never happen again."

Much of our communications are fleeting and with unknown persons. The best communication model is the orchestra. In the orchestra, all the musicians have their sheet music, and all conform simultaneously to the direct communication methods of the conductor. Everyone has a role, and everyone has a duty to conform, and everyone knows what to expect. The orchestra then communicates their music to the audience. But even in this case, the listener, the audience, interprets the communication in a myriad of ways. Communication is a very difficult and complex process. It's no wonder we have libraries full of law books trying to assist us in interpreting the meaning of the law. The courts interpret the law. Often, the courts will decide cases based solely on how they define one word. The words "arrest," "unreasonable," "search," "detain," "reasonable," "pornography," "ownership," "custodial," "contract," have all been laboriously, painstakingly, and famously defined by the courts for our legal system. In order for the legal system to work, we need to know what these words mean.

Also, every person is different. We, as investigators, analysts, parents, attorneys, professional and financial experts, have to calibrate to each person we're listening to or watching in order to truly communicate. The calibration process is very important. It's during that process, while we observe or ask our preliminary less important questions like, "Where do you live?"

"What is your date of birth?," etc. that we determine the person's unique manner of communicating. By observing the person's pitch, pace, rhythm, breathing, glances, and facial expressions when responding to these seemingly innocuous questions, we can corroborate and use that information to help determine whether we're getting partial truths when asking the important questions. Calibration is important and it's difficult to master. It takes time and practice.

Our unique Alvin, our individual and unique communication process, is controlled by our individual consciences. In my axe story, it was my Alvin who concocted the successful response, "I fell on Mr. Tuinier's driveway." It also took Alvin a little extra processing time to come up with that brilliant escape from almost certain punishment. It takes more processing time to tell a partial truth, than to tell the truth. It's physics and physiological. There are more variables to consider when telling a partial truth since you must consider the whole truth, then concoct a well-crafted message that contains only a part of that truth without revealing the whole truth. That extra processing time creates a pause, a track. And just like a crime scene, that track is there for the Trained Observer to get.

It is Alvin who tells the truth. It is also Alvin who concocts the partial truth. Alvin resists telling a complete lie. And Alvin is very good at it — he's had a lifetime to develop, experiment, and practice. Alvin is precise, not haphazard, and carefully, precisely, selects the words and all the other communication variables to produce the best communicative solution for the moment. If we need to tell a partial truth, we will direct our Alvin to create a message that will suggest one thing, while saying another. Remember, Alvin is precise and crafty. Never, ever underestimate Alvin.

As stated earlier, we begin learning how to lie at the age of 2 years, if not sooner. Alvin works overtime to enable us to avoid punishment, to tell partial truths. Alvin, using our formative years and the memories of our childhood, keeps us from telling complete lies. And, thus, allows us to live with ourselves, our consciences, and with each other. He's free and comes with the package. Mother Nature approves of the process too, or it would have eliminated it over time. The story of Adam and Eve comes to mind. I've never lost sleep because of the partial truth I told to my mom. Partial truths help soothe the conscience.

```
"I've said it for seven years. I haven't doped."
                                    —Lance Armstrong
```

Here's the classic introduction to a weak, unreliable denial: "I've said it . . .". Or another variation, "I can say . . ." One needs to go back to the original "denial" to see what was originally said. Chances are very good that he didn't say, "I haven't doped," or even more improbably, "I didn't dope." I say more improbably because "I didn't dope" is more simple and direct and it contains a contraction. More on contractions later.

DENIALS

Simplicity is the key to getting the truth. The truthful and complete statement or response is simple, clear, precise, and direct. Anything else is suspicious.

I have fond memories of my old hometown and my childhood. Memories are very important to us. They serve as our foundation. They affect everything we do, don't do, and think about doing - when we do it, where we do it, if we do it, and how we do it. And memories have great influence on how we communicate — to include how we hear things, how we interpret what we hear, how we evaluate it, how we filter it. Our memories largely determine how we think. Memories are the foundation for bias — and just about everything else. And memories are physical.

It's event memories that teach us how to tell partial truths. We learned at a very young age that if we tell partial truths, we may avoid punishment. If we tell "little lies" (partial truths like my axe story) we might get away with our transgressions. We can wiggle through to minimize punishment by telling the least amount of truth possible to convince the listener we're telling the whole truth. A little truth goes a long way. Even President Lincoln used a partial truth to help pass the Thirteenth Amendment:

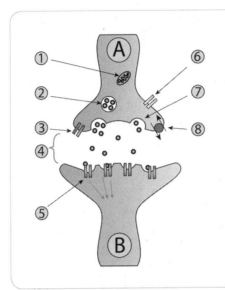

Memories are stored as new connections between neurons. When you hit your first homerun, danced your first dance, experienced your first kiss—neuron connections formed to include the smells, sounds, physical reactions, feelings, and sights of those moments. You lived those moments. Memories are real!

Lies don't have these connections.

Graphic Wikipedia

Just prior to Abolition of Slavery vote—Thirteenth Amendment January 31, 1865

A rumor was circulating in the House that peace commissioners were en route to Washington . . . Representative Ashley requested authorization to contradict the rumor . . .

"So far as I know, there are no peace commissioners in the city, or likely to be in it."
—President Abraham Lincoln, January 31, 1865

Lincoln wanted to seize the window of opportunity he had in front of him to pass the Thirteenth Amendment. On January 31, 1865, the window was open and ready. So, he told a partial truth to satiate the inquisitors and to allow the vote to take place. Lincoln omitted the fact he was detaining the peace commissioners in a southern city, keeping them from making it to Washington, D.C. Catholics would call this a sin of "omission" instead of a sin of "commission."

So, if we just don't say it, how can it be a lie? A lie isn't a lie unless you say it or write it. Right? So, if you stay silent about your acts or observations, avoid telling the whole truth, you might avoid punishment, or like Lincoln, further your agenda, and accomplish your goal. It's a win-win!

I see no evil....
I hear no evil....
I speak no evil.

However, by telling a partial truth you intentionally mislead the listener. And that is deception, pure and simple. So, it's not that easy to find a win-win. We're stuck with our consciences, deeply embedded in our Alvin. When it comes down to it, telling partial truths (lies) is hard. Alvin works very hard. His work, by necessity, has to be precise and error free. Crafting partial truths is tough. Telling a partial truth is more stressful (because it is much more complex) than telling the whole truth. Alvin, though, evolved into a well-developed, very formidable, crafty, partial-truth-producing marvel.

"It's harder to lie,
than to tell the truth."
    —PBS Nova, 10/17/12, Can Science Stop Crime?

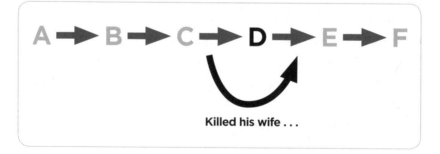

If I'm telling you what happened yesterday, I recite to you various events that happened. I start with A, then go to B, then to C, etc. The trouble is, I killed my wife yesterday between events C and E. To create a partial truth, my Alvin needs to create, construct something, somehow to connect event C with event E without raising suspicion, making the story sound logical and making the event flow seamlessly. That's a very difficult process. Remember, memories are physical, lies aren't. Memories have physical properties that allow me to rely upon them — lies don't. I'm under a lot of stress when creating this link and I have to remember exactly how I construct everything. Tracks are left in the process.

When you're writing a letter to your boss or to a judge or someone of authority, you don't use contractions. It's always "I do not believe," and never "I don't believe." That's because it is a more formal setting, and you are under greater stress when writing to your boss or a judge than you are when writing to your wife (maybe not a good example — but you know what I mean). The use of contractions, therefore, is usually a sign the user is under less stress.

Contractions are elisions, a shortened form of a word. "It is" becomes it's. "Was not" becomes wasn't. "Did not" becomes didn't. We expect that with more stress, there is more formality and with more stress, less use of contractions. Now that is not to say that a formal denial, " I did not do it," is not reliable. Simply, the denial, " I didn't do it," is usually more reliable. The use of more formal language, more of what I call "artillery," is often used to convince you that he/she is telling the truth. When President Clinton addressed the American Public, he used a lot of artillery:

CLINTON: 'LISTEN TO ME'

Clinton's emphatic denial Monday came after several days of silence on the allegations, even as tension was building for him to explain any relationship with Lewinsky.

Wagging his finger for emphasis at the end of a White House ceremony on child care, Clinton stared into a bank of TV cameras and declared, "I want to say one thing to the American people. I want you to listen to me. I'm going to say this again. I did not have sexual relations with that woman, Miss Lewinsky."

The dramatic 20-second statement buoyed Clinton's supporters and riveted attention on what Lewinsky would tell Starr's grand jury.

"I never told anybody to lie," Clinton said in the remarkable White House statement. "Not a single time. Never. These allegations are false and I need to go back to work for the American people."

LEWINSKY MAKES OFFER
Lewinsky's attorney, William Ginsburg,

Note the "Wagging his finger," "Clinton stared into," and then the biggie: "I want to say one thing…." And "I'm going to say this again." (Introductions will be addressed in Chapter 6.) But do you see any contractions? Yes, there is one. However, take note of where it is. It is in the statement, "I'm going to say this again." He can be relaxed when he says that because he has said that before. There is no stress in that statement because it is true — he did say that before. So we can disregard this contraction. But there are no other contractions. When someone isn't telling the truth and they want to convince you they are, they pull out all the tools in their toolbox: stares, forcefulness, loudness, intimidation, formality, structure, stress, finger pointing, etc. You need to remember this:

- The simpler the denial the better.
- If she doesn't deny it, she did it.
- If he didn't answer the question, he did.

Let's look at Jerry Sandusky's first formal statement following his conviction for pedophilic activity.

```
Jerry Sandusky Statement  10/2012 (partial)

"I'm responding to the worst loss of my
life. First, I looked at myself. Over and
over, I asked why? Why didn't we have a
fair opportunity to prepare for trial? Why
have so many people suffered as a result of
false allegations? What's the purpose?
                          why no "these"?
Maybe it will help others, some vulnerable
children who could be abused might not be as a
result of all the publicity. That would be
nice, but I'm not sure about it.
I would cherish the opportunity to become a
candle for others, as they have been a light
for me. They could take away my life, they
could make me out as a monster, they could
treat me as a monster, but they can't take away
my heart. In my heart, I know I did not do
these alleged disgusting acts.
                          (didn't??)
```

Notice he starts his statement with the contraction, "I'm." Further, notice all the contractions used (highlighted) until the last sentence of the last paragraph, where he begins his "denial." Also note that denials are more believable if they are early in a "denial statement." At the point of his "denial," he doesn't use a contraction, despite using many earlier. Not only is the denial late in his statement, it is preceded by a telling introduction, "In my heart," and "I know." Introductions are fatal to denials. Let's learn about them and how important they are.

```
"I am absolutely, 100% not guilty."
                          — O.J. Simpson
```

The words "not guilty" have a lot of "wiggle" room in them. It can take months of court action to determine if some-one is not guilty. So, his statement is true — he is not guilty, until proven guilty.

Chapter 6

INTRODUCTIONS

Before you read a word of this book, your thoughts were contaminated.

You have prejudices, biases, and maybe even more. We all have them. The very title of this book contaminates

An introduction is anything that qualifies a statement.

all that follows. The color, the size, the look of this book, the price — all contaminate. We need to be fully aware of our innate limitations. We need to know, going in, that we hold predispositions that will filter, cloud, obfuscate, and prevent us from seeing, sensing the facts. That's why kids see things differently than we do. They haven't developed those prejudices and filters that we've developed over time. As stated before, kids are excellent receivers.

Introductions are anything that qualifies the statement. Introductions can follow the statement or response, as in a retroactive introduction (see the Herman Cain example below). Note that this definition is not limited to words.

If you're selling a product or service, how do you begin to ask the very first question that can lead to a sale? Do you put much time into properly framing it? The first question will largely determine what follows. You need to make sure your first question is clear, simple, precisely constructed, and unrestrictive.

Clear means that both you and the client must mutually understand each and every word you use. If you ask, "Do you wish to invest in securities?" — you need to know that both you and the client identically define the word "securities." If you ask, "How may I help you?" — you need to understand you are restricting responses. At first glance it seems to be perfect and harmless, but let's look closer. The client may not know how you can help them, so their response may be not what it would have been with a different, less restrictive introduction. These may sound like very trivial points, but they're not.

If you ask, "Where do you see yourself in the future?" — that, too, may be restrictive and threatening. We simply can't rely on anything in the future. The client may be threatened by that question because they don't want to divulge to a stranger what their dreams are. A better, unrestrictive and open question to a prospective client who has walked into your office might be, "What brings you here?"

As stated before, introductions can follow the statement. Let's look at Herman Cain's denial of sexual harassment charges:

```
"I have never sexually harassed anyone, let's
say that, . . ."
                  — Presidential candidate, Herman Cain
                                         10/31/2011.
```

His statement is actually followed by an introduction, something I've already called a retroactive introduction. Besides his use of the passive voice in his denial, his retroactive introduction adds further evidence of deception. You simply cannot rely on this denial.

Look at a Q & A between NBC's Ann Curry and Iran's President Hassan Rouhani (NBC News Posted 9/18/2013):

"CURRY: Can you say that Iran will not build a nuclear weapon under any circumstances whatsoever?

ROUHANI: The answer to this question is quite obvious. We have time and again said that under no circumstances would we seek any weapons of mass destruction, including nuclear weapons, nor will we ever."

The question is poorly structured. The "Can you say" is fraught with wiggle room, opportunity for vagueness, and offers the politician an easy way out. Also, note his answer. "The answer to this question" is not necessarily his answer. He also says, "We have time and again said . . ." Again, that is not his answer. Also note that he doesn't own it. Had he said "My answer to this question," I would give it more weight and credibility, but since he doesn't when he had the opportunity to do so, I won't. And neither should the American government.

In Chapter 3, I talk about President Clinton's denial involving Monica Lewinski. He uses the introduction, "I want to say one thing to the American people." He also states, "I'm going to say this again." These are introductions. <u>When you see introductions like these, you can't rely on what follows</u>. The speaker is warning you and you need to look at these introductions in a literal way. Mr. Clinton's Alvin constructed that introduction. The introduction, "I can tell you this," gives the speaker the latitude to tell you anything he/she wants because they told you they were going to "tell you this!" Alvin looks at that as a partial truth. Anything that follows is, therefore, unreliable because they, in fact, did tell you that (whatever they told you). Remember the partial truth — the introduction paves the way for the partial truth.

Take a look at this statement (in particular, the introduction he uses) by then Congressman Weiner:

> BLITZER: Have you ever taken a picture of yourself like this?
> ► WEINER: I can tell you this, that there are — I have photographs. I don't know what photographs are out there in the world of me. I don't know what things have been manipulated and doctored, and we're going to try to find out what happened. But the most important reason I want to find out what happened is to make sure it doesn't happen again. Obviously, somebody got access to my account; that's bad. They sent a picture that makes fun of the gam Weiner. I get it. You know, touche, Dr. Moriarty, you got me. At the time it happened, I tweeted right away that I got the joke and I continued on with my life. And I think that, frankly, that's what I would encourage everyone to do. I don't believe that this is a big federal issue, but people are free to pursue it if they like.

See Congressman Weiner's introduction: "I can tell you this . . ." You cannot rely on what follows with that kind of introduction. Then we must ask ourselves, "Why is such an introduction necessary?" He could have answered, simply, "I have photographs." But he didn't. And the fact that he didn't, when he could have, is deceptive.

- *Be suspicious of denials (or anything else!) with *introductions:*
- "I can tell you this . . ." *You can't rely on what follows.*

"She was not choked. She was not punched."
—Pastor Dollar 6/10/12

In this case, Pastor Dollar constructs his denial as a declaration, a statement which is not a denial since he doesn't say "I" or "me." He could have said, "I did not choke her; I did not punch her," but he didn't. There is no attribution to Pastor Dollar — it's a form of an introduction to a denial that isn't a denial.

- "I can say . . ." *You can't rely on what follows.*
- "I said this before . . ." *You can't rely on what follows.*
- "I wasn't raised to . . ." *You can't rely on what follows.*
- "I am innocent . . ." *You can't rely on 'wiggle' words. <u>Wiggle words are words that someone can interpret their own way to gain an advantage.</u>*
- "I am absolutely, 100% not guilty." *O.J. is absolutely, 100% not guilty until proven guilty. It's the truth.*
- "I have never sexually harassed anyone, let's say that." *Not simple, not direct, and a bonus!! A retroactive introduction!!!*
- "I could never hurt Susan or my sons." Josh Powell *"I will never" is stronger.*
- "I've said it for 7 years — I haven't doped" *You can't rely on what follows.*
- "I'm not a murderer." Amanda Knox 4/30/2013. *Present tense and not precise. "I did not kill . . ." is more direct; "murderer" has a lot of wiggle.*

One simply cannot rely on statements preceded or followed by introductions or qualifiers. That doesn't necessarily mean the statement is untrue, you just can't rely on it. Be suspicious, and be observant. These introductions/qualifiers can be very subtle, almost imperceptible, especially in verbal discourse. That is by design. The objective is to say it, and make you believe it at the same time.

Notice the definition of introductions: *Anything that qualifies the statement.* The introduction doesn't have to be verbal. Pauses, eye movements, a shift in position, a nod of the head, feet crossed over, an exhalation of breath all are introductions. Remember my *almost imperceptible pause* in the axe story? That was an introduction. It takes any form and carries the same force. Be observant. Be a Trained Observer. And, remember the introduction/qualifier can *follow* the statement, as in:

"I have never sexually harassed anyone, let's say that."

> — Presidential candidate, Herman Cain
> 10/31/2011 on Fox News.

Jerry Sandusky Statement   10/2012 (partial)

"I'm responding to the worst *loss* of my life. First, I looked at myself. Over and over, I asked why? Why didn't we have a fair opportunity to prepare for trial? Why have so many people suffered as a result of *false allegations*? What's the purpose?

why no "these"?

Maybe it will help others, some vulnerable children who could be abused might not be as a result of all the publicity. That would be nice, but I'm not sure about it. I would cherish the opportunity to become a candle for others, as they have been a light for me. They could take away my life, they could make me out as a monster, they could treat me as a monster, but they can't take away my heart. In my heart, I know I did not do these alleged disgusting acts.

(didn't??)

When Anthony Weiner looks down before he answers a question, when Bill Clinton stares at the cameras before his statement, when your daughter looks away just after you ask the question, *"Where were you last night?"* — all of those are introductions. They may portend that a partial truth is about to follow. Introductions don't always mean that, but, again, once you calibrate to the person responding, you will get the message. *Better*: You will be able to better interpret the response. Again, let's take a look at Jerry Sandusky's statement:

```
"In my heart, I know I did not do these alleged
disgusting acts."
                        — Jerry Sandusky 10/2012
              (part of statement after conviction)
```

There are all kinds of problems with this weak, inadequate denial. The introduction, "In my heart," taints all that follows. Followed by the "I know," brings extra baggage. Finally, the absence of a contraction for "I did not," when his earlier sentences in this statement contained numerous contractions begs the question why no contraction on the all-important denial? The answer to all of these issues is — his Alvin wouldn't allow it.

Chapter 7

CONTAMINATION (FRUIT OF THE POISONOUS TREE)

Precision is the nemesis of deception. Promote verbosity and volume using mutually understood words, but look for simplicity and precision to get the truth.

"Five frogs are sitting on a log. Four decide to jump off. How many are left?"

Five, because *deciding* is not doing.

This, obviously, isn't a deception-detecting question. It's a trick question. But it shows you need to read all the words. Nothing is trivial and nothing is haphazard. Nothing is without purpose. Telling partial lies is all about deception, subtlety, and distraction. Let nothing go unexamined. *Even nothing has to be examined.*

Do you think the Miranda Rights contaminate the subject's response? Police officers are forced to read these rights to the suspect when he/she is in custody.

- You have the right to remain silent.
- Anything you can and will be used against you in a court of law.
- You have the right to consult an attorney before speaking to the police and to have an attorney present during questioning now or in the future.

- If you cannot afford an attorney, one will be appointed for you before any questioning, if you wish.
- If you decide to answer any questions now, without an attorney present, you will still have the right to stop answering at any time until you talk to an attorney.
- Knowing and understanding your rights as I have explained them to you, are you willing to answer my questions without an attorney present?

Yes. However, a lot depends on how the Miranda Rights are delivered and how the introduction is delivered. If the rights are given matter-of-factly and cold, the subject may well ask for an attorney. If the rights, as I used to, were given warmly and openly and in such a way as to gain the confidence and trust of the subject, then maybe the subject will talk. I used this approach often, as I did, and still do, believe the subject was often better off being truthful and using this truth-purge as a turning point in his life to get back on track.

Most contamination is not forced, it is chosen. We can't eliminate it, but we can greatly reduce it. Contamination is the enemy of truth. For investigators, attorneys, parents, due diligence efforts, analysis of executive statements, and any other fact-finding endeavor, this question must be asked:

> **Have I, in any way, affected the subject's future responses?**

If your answer is "yes," then you've contaminated the statement.

By nodding in agreement when the subject responds, have I affected his/her future responses in any way? Have the words in my question altered the subject's response? If I worded the question differently, would I get a different story? Do we both know what each other is really saying? Am I making assumptions about what he is saying? When I take notes, am I communicating something that will impact the subject's response or future responses? Does my question structure itself limit the information the subject would have otherwise provided me?

Apple's Dictionary definition of the verb, contaminate, is: "to make (something) impure by exposure to or addition of a poisonous or polluting substance."

So, we need to make sure our actions, sentence structure, behavior, voice inflections, expressions, attitudes, don't change what the subject would tell us without those influences. You can see, a proper questioning process is very complex. It takes proper training, productive experience, patience, and introspection.

TV detective shows always show two detectives interviewing suspects or witnesses. Many police departments send two detectives to conduct interviews. Detectives like to work together and many think they obtain more information because two eyes and ears are better than one. Detectives Phillip Lange and Thomas Vannatter of the LAPD interviewed O.J. Simpson together on 6/13/1994 when Simpson flew back to LA from Chicago within days after the murder of Nicole Simpson and Ronald Goldman. It was always Jack Webb "Joe Friday" and his sidekick "Bill Gannon" played by Harry Morgan. Unfortunately, the presence of two detectives insures the interview will be contaminated. Actually all interviews are contaminated, but two detectives insure there will be much more contamination than necessary. Contamination all too often leads to bad confessions, bad facts, bad evidence, and bad convictions. In the case of business decisions, contamination leads to bad financial decisions. And, while I'm at it, I'll say that contamination is the mother of all bad decisions. Make sure you do your best to eliminate contamination.

In the LAPD interview of O.J. Simpson, there are many examples where one detective interrupted the thought process of the other, leading to responses not properly pursued and details not disclosed. O.J. knew he could provide unclear or vague responses and not be forced to explain them.

Interviews need to be conducted one-on-one. The CIA, Mossad, and KGB all know this. They do this for a reason: to eliminate as much contamination as possible. And to make sure answers are thoroughly pursued, producing precise details that can be corroborated to help determine the truth.

Every movement, every nuance in language, every furtive glance, every note taken, and every other observable action or inaction communicates something to the suspect. That communication will contaminate future responses. The key is to minimize contamination.

The question structure determines the response. Structure your initial questions to promote open, uncontaminated responses. Use only mutually understood words. Then look for precision, accuracy, simplicity, and directness. You then focus on where those are missing.

The worst mistake investigators, business people, or attorneys make is to ask poorly constructed questions. "He who speaks first loses." That's true in bargaining, and it's true in finding facts.

A poorly constructed question contaminates what follows. In fact, every question contaminates what follows. But a carefully constructed first question minimizes the contamination. The very first question is the most important, the most critical. Because it is the seed for all that follows. If poison is produced, it is because of that seed.

First questions need to be short and simple and contain only words that are mutually understood by all the participants in the questioning. Nothing else is acceptable. Adequate first questions are:

Tell me what happened.
Do you know why you're here?
What happened?

And even the words in those questions can be misunderstood. The finder of facts needs to know quickly if the subject completely understands what is being asked. That can be accomplished by asking the following question before the subject responds:

What do you think I mean when I ask you "Tell me what happened?"
What do you think I mean when I ask you "Do you know why you're here?"
What do you think I mean when I ask you "What happened?"

Again, I often conduct interviews by writing out the questions in one color ink and ask the subject to respond in writing in another color ink. That way there is less doubt about what was asked and how it was answered. Further, I do this on plain white copy paper — no structure, no lines, and no limit to the number of pages of response. Everything the subject writes provides clues and facts to help determine the truth.

I once investigated missing money at a bank. I made the mistake of asking one of the bank executives "Do you know why you're here?" without first determining if we both understood the question. He responded, in writing, and in lengthy fashion, to tell me how he applied for his current position and why! So, you can never truly know how your words are being interpreted until you ask! True communication is very, very difficult and complex.

CONTAMINATING QUESTIONS

Can you say unequivocally that . . . ?
Larry King to Lance Armstrong
Sure, I can say anything — that doesn't make it true.

What *would* you say . . . ?
What I would say doesn't necessarily mean I would say it.

Did you kill your wife or didn't you?
I can answer this "yes" or "no" and you would not know if I killed my wife.

Are you *lying* to me?
By now you know the word "lying" is fraught with ambiguity, and is subject to a myriad of definitions.

Is it *true* that you . . . ?
Same response as the immediate above. What constitutes "true?" What you believe or what I believe?

I swear that I will tell the truth . . .
Our judicial system is based on a poorly worded oath.

Are you innocent?
What do you think?

By now you have a feeling for the ambiguity of words. Ambiguity leads to wiggle room. Wiggle room (words that can be interpreted to allow someone to gain advantage) allows the responder to conceal the truth. A wiggle word can be used to deceive. **Construct your questions (and look for responses) that contain no wiggle words.** The only way to eliminate the possibility of wiggle words is to openly discuss the meaning of words used.

Interviews need to be treated like crime scenes. Every effort should be made to minimize contamination. Again, every question contaminates the response. It's like every action has an equal and opposite reaction. The best interview is a one-on-one, not two or more on one. The goal in an interview or interrogation is to get the truth. The truth can only be obtained through a questioning strategy that minimizes contamination.

"Can you say unequivocally that you have never used an illegal substance? Ever?"

CNN Larry King interview of Lance Armstrong, 8/25/2005

Lance's response: "Listen, I've said it for seven years. I've said it for longer than seven years. I have never doped."

In the movie, In Her Shoes, actress Shirley McLain is asked:

"Do you have any children?"
"No, I don't have any children."

She did have children at one time, but both died. Later she clarified: "I didn't say, I didn't have any children."

Predisposition is a huge filter that inhibits seeing and feeling the truth. If you are predisposed, you will see only those things you wish to see. And you will not see, hear, feel, or smell those things you don't wish to know. This is true in racism, and it's true in truth-getting. Obviously, we cannot completely control our predispositions. But, simply being aware of our predispositions can go a long way to helping us see the truth.

Chapter 8

MINIMIZING CONTAMINATION

Hunters know there is a predator in the area when the birds stop chirping. If the interviewer pauses before asking the next question, the interviewee

Even the absence of contamination can contaminate.

knows something happened. *The absence of contamination can contaminate.*

If there is noise in the interview room, that noise may contaminate the subject's responses. So, what if that noise suddenly stops halfway into the interview? The absence of that noise may now contaminate future responses.

So, how do you minimize contamination in the question process? The object of any interview is to obtain a Pristine Version (PV). I define the PV simply as the subject's uncontaminated description of the event(s). The PV is obtained by asking a single open question to determine what the subject has to say about what happened, and nothing more. In the PV, the subject will tell what he/she thinks is most important, and omit those things which he deems unimportant.

For emphasis and as stated before, for the PV to be most valuable, the first question has to be very carefully constructed. The first question is the most important part of the interview. The interviewer needs to be assured the subject being interviewed has a mutual understanding of the words in the questions. The first question needs to be short, simple, and open. The purpose of the open first question is to elicit a lengthy response from the subject. The interviewer then is able to gain insight into the subject's vocabulary, thought process, rhythm, pace, prosody, whether he/she uses elision (contractions), writing or breathing habits, facial expressions, sounds, intonation, incantation, articulation, eye and eyebrow movements, blinking, etc. The first question provides the interviewer insight into how to calibrate the interview strategy to the individual. As stated earlier, a good first question is, "Tell me what happened," or "Why do you think you're here?"

Calibrating your strategy to the subject is important. You need to know the individual before you can truly communicate. That's why that first question is so important. Not only do you set the tone for the interview, the response serves as the foundation for all that follows. I use the first question to elicit the subject's response, then use the subject's words (vocabulary) in my subsequent questions only after first defining those words. If I need to ask a question using a word the subject hasn't used, I first define that word or ask the subject to define it for me so that there is no wiggle room, no misunderstanding in the meaning of the words I use. That is where contamination begins. It starts when the meaning of the words is not fully understood by both parties.

Take the forensic interview process that is supposed to be followed when children are accusing an adult of an illegal act. These interviews should be video recorded with good sound to make sure we can review these statements later to analyze and help determine the validity of the statement. Contamination, of all sorts, has to be eliminated. Small children can be intimidated or distracted by the slightest sounds and sights. As stated before, they are very good receivers. What they say or do can be easily manipulated by intentional or unintentional adult actions and inactions. There is much we are learning as to what goes on in the child's mind. If the very first question leads to contamination, the whole interview is suspect. A child's interview has to be very carefully designed so the child tells what the child knows, not what the interviewer thinks the child knows, or what any other party thinks the child knows, or what the child might think the interviewer wants or what anybody else wants. Many people of influence may have already talked to the child, already creating possible contamination of what the child is about to tell the interviewer. The interviewer needs to be able to minimize those influences, identify them if they are present, and know how to obtain the best imperfect PV as possible.

When the subject can write, even with older children, I often conduct the statement process using an old fashioned method — exchanging notes. I write out my question (by hand) and request the subject respond in the same way — in his own handwriting. I use unstructured, plain, white paper — copy paper and lots of it. The environment I want to create is that there are no time limits, no paper limits, no distractions, and no restrictions — just let the thoughts flow. I often leave the room after writing the first question to further minimize contamination. There are forces you can take advantage of by doing so. A subject, alone in a silent room with his thoughts, writing on plain sheets of paper can do wonders for illumination and thought flow. Several good things result from this process:

1. You will get a feel for the subject's intelligence, ability to communicate, spelling issues, language issues, and all sorts of things. Sometimes you can see the stress in the subject's handwriting, which may lead to further inquiry and exploration. See the example below.

2. Again, the first question is the most important. You need to spend time to formulate that question. Most polygraph examinations that are deemed flawed are because of the

way the examiner constructed the critical question. You need to make sure both you and the subject agree upon the meaning of each and every word. That goes for the subject's responses as well. You, as the interviewer, have to know what the subject means when she says, "I slipped and fell...." You may assume you know, but never assume. Have the subject define the words they use. That is not to say you need to define "each and every word." But it does mean you need to make sure you are not assuming the meaning of any words. Likewise, you must define your words as well. *Wiggle* words are a killer and can ruin truth-getting.

Let's say I ask a subject, "Did you kill your wife?" without defining the word "kill." Now, this subject may be a person who feels only God can give life and only God can take life. How then could he "kill" his wife? You never know what Alvin will rely upon. So, your first question before this one should be, "John, before I ask the next question I first want to make sure we both understand what it means. If I were to use the word "kill," what would that word mean to you." Or, maybe we have a subject who believes that only the Medical Examiner knows what killed the victim. Can I answer "No" to the "Did you kill your wife?" question if I don't know what killed my wife? I know, this can go on and on, but you get the point. We need to eliminate the *wiggle* in our words <u>and</u> the subject's words. Then, once you have a common understanding of the key word, you can use it. Remember President Clinton's statement, "I did not have sexual relations with that woman, Ms. Lewinsky."

3. The first question is open and without boundaries. There are several reasons for this. In the example below, the subject was told by his supervisors before my interview why he was being interviewed — his ex-wife accused him of forging her signature on checks made out to her and pocketing the

money. But what if the supervisor hadn't contaminated my interview by simply telling the subject an investigator wants to talk to you. What kind of response would I have received to the question: "Tell me why you are here?" I'll never know.

But, in this case, I simply requested, "Tell me what happened."

> the checks. I called my ex-wife at her place of work and told her about the check and asked her to meet me at the bank. She stated she could not leave work during the day. She had recently started an new job and had already missed some time. I asked her to meet me at the bank on Saturday and she stated she had plans and would not be able to. I asked her what I was supposed to do. She said to sign her name and to deposit it in the ATM machine and that it would go through fine. She said if there were any questions or problems that she would clear it up. The same scenerio happened with subsequent checks. Now, we are in the middle of

4. Just look at his statement. I've minimized contamination. And I know there is little that I have said or done to influence his statement. Note the handwriting and how fluent and easy the handwriting is in the beginning of the paragraph. Then see what appears to be a change in the handwriting. You can't miss it. Following "It is harder to lie than to tell the truth", the stress of telling partial truths shows in the handwriting. It's much like a polygraph, where stress is shown in the graphs. In this case, the subject's handwriting reveals a great deal of stress when he states, "She said to sign her name...." That's not a coincidence and it is revealing. Using this information and the confidence that the subject was troubled when stating the critical authorization by his wife to sign her name,

I obtained a confession from the subject. While his ex-wife had given him permission before to sign her name on checks, she did not give permission to sign her name on these recent checks. He was terminated.

5. I constructed my subsequent questions to him using his own language, but only after defining it. For example, my next question in this interview was, "You said 'She said to sign her name.' - Please tell me about that." I then forced him to provide more partial truths to corroborate his original falsehood. Eventually, like sand through an hourglass, he ran out of room, logic, reasoning, excuses, and stamina. The absurdity of his story and reasoning lead to the confession, and what everyone eventually finds most comfortable — telling the truth. Like in nature, water seeks its own level. We lower our stress by telling the truth.

"Anyone who knows me, or who worked with me, would know that I wouldn't, and more importantly that I didn't, do anything to damage the Milly Dowler investigation."
        — Andy Coulson, The Guardian, 7/24/2012

Is that a good denial — or is it The Weasel Effect? (see Chapter 10).

Chapter 9

INTENTIONAL AND SUSTAINING CONTAMINATION

Up to now, we've discussed the need for finding the truth, the facts. But, what if your objective isn't to find the truth or the facts? What if your objective is to persuade the subject to buy something, or sell something, or not to buy something? Or, you wish to have the subject say something that is helpful to your case. This may be neither unethical nor illegal.

Attorneys, salespeople, marketing strategists, psychologists, professional athletes, gamblers, magicians, and just about everybody will employ this approach all the time. We can create a different paradigm. We can flip the non-contamination approach and create an approach that induces contamination. Intentional contamination can help prove or enhance your position or your client's position.

Leading questions are a surefire method to contaminate the response. Here's the classic:

"So, when did you stop beating your wife?"

I always wanted to ask a physicist the contaminating question, "What time is it?" I would expect that question to disable him for some time, causing his eyes to glaze over and have a far-off look.

Or how about these:

"Tell me, are there problems in your relationship with your wife?"

"Will you ever stop lying to my questions?"

"Didn't he appear to be firing the weapon?"

"You were at the scene that night, weren't you?"

"How much will the stock go up next year?"

"You are going to tell the truth, aren't you?"

I just know Miguel Cabrera intentionally swings poorly at a not too perfect pitch, to entice the pitcher into throwing the same pitch and then hitting it out of the park.

How about the propaganda various intelligence agencies produce to assist in attaining their goals? Magicians distract you in order to perform their magic. They make you think you're seeing one thing, to distract you or contaminate what you think you see to further their goals of deception. Gamblers make their money through deception and observation. A gambler's bluff doesn't work without proper foundation. He needs to convince the other players he has something when, in fact, he doesn't. Fight contestants often try to win the about-to-be-fought contest through a pre-fight intimidation process — although I'm not sure that contamination process works. Contamination has its place.

Listen to college and professional coaches when talking about prospective opponents. They always praise the opponents. That's contamination.

You can also intentionally contaminate by the way you dress. If I want to return an item at a store where the return might be questionable (beyond the 60 days, for example), I will dress in a blue suit with a red tie to portray myself as important, knowledgeable, and not easy to dissuade. If I try to do the same dressed in jeans and an old sweatshirt I won't be as successful — guaranteed!

What happens when you visit a doctor, lawyer, accountant, or a financial consultant? You sit in her office to wait to see her and all you see are trappings of success, luxurious furniture, carpeting, and ornaments, plaques showing awards and commendations. How does that impact her credibility? Are they using contamination to their benefit? What would happen if, in the alternative, the office setting were an office that was unkempt, worn furniture, spots on the carpet, etc.?

Let's look at the scientific method, a well-proven model to prove that something doesn't happen simply due to chance or expectation. Aspects of that model are directed toward eliminating the "placebo effect," an improvement in health or condition not due to the treatment or medication. If you think, you will. Our mental gymnastics are a form of intentional contamination.

Your first impressions can make or break you. Remember, a first impression lays there in your client's mind affecting all that follows. If the impression is a good one, the client is more likely to accept you, to respect you, and to follow you. We've talked about how our minds filter out important information simply because it doesn't fit our expectations, or our desires, or our beliefs. First impressions work the same way.

Let's look at our previous example where Wolf Blitzer asked Congressman Weiner:

BLITZER: Have you ever taken a picture of yourself like this?
WEINER: I can tell you this, that there are — I have photographs. I don't know what photographs are out there in the world of me. I don't know what things have been manipulated and doctored, and we're going to try to find out what happened. But the most important reason I want to find out what happened is to make sure it doesn't happen again. Obviously, somebody got access to my account; that's bad. They sent a picture that makes fun of the gam Weiner. I get it. You know, touche, Dr. Moriarty, you got me. At the time it happened, I tweeted right away that I got the joke and I continued on with my life. And I think that, frankly, that's what I would encourage everyone to do. I don't believe that this is a big federal issue, but people are free to pursue it if they like.

What might Congressman Weiner's response been had Wolf asked: "Tell me about this photograph." Or "Did you take this picture?"

Let's say an attorney is asking a subject (defendant) questions about her assets, to help identify assets that could be useful in a lawsuit. In this case, let's assume the woman is not educated, is unsophisticated in economics and finance, and has a somewhat limited vocabulary. What if he phrases his question like this (I've seen these in depositions!)?

- "What assets do you have?"
- "What assets without liens do you have?"
- "Do you have any chattel?"
- "Do you have any chattel mortgages?"
- "Do you have any intangible assets?"
- "Do you have any real property?"

The woman may not even know what an asset is. Words that seem to have universal meaning are not universally understood. We often use words that come secondhand to us because we use them so often. Take medical doctors for example. We all know how they talk! But, how do we expect the woman to answer?

She may answer "No." What does that mean? Look at all the ways you could interpret that answer. If you assume she knows what you've asked, you may assume she lied if you know otherwise. She may have knowledge and is able to hide in the "wiggle" room you just created by asking the question in the way you did. Let's assume she does know, but has a plausible reason for Alvin to allow her to say "no." You may assume she really doesn't have those assets. You may base a legal strategy on the basis of that answer and waste valuable time and money. Yes, one may argue later that the subject answered "No" and may try to proffer the argument the subject intentionally tried to deceive, but that may serve only to make the attorney look bad. On the other hand, it may slip by undetected and entered as evidence.

But, really, we need to take the time to make sure the subject knows the words we're using in our questions, especially in legal discovery processes. Otherwise, we run the risk of missing key information. Remember, it's there. We just have to find it. And you won't find it if you allow the subject "wiggle" room. The subject will take advantage and give you a partial truth. We need to get the whole truth. That's where the hidden assets are.

Let's say the reverse is true, where the attorney or officer asking the question is not as well versed as the subject answering the question. This happens all the time in litigations involving patents, criminal cases, bankruptcies, and others. Experts are experts for a reason. They know more about what they're experts in than the attorneys asking the questions. So, when an expert provides an opinion, we need to really hone in on the words they use, and define them so everyone understands. Just like deceptive people, experts can hide the truth in semantics, in their esoteric language, to the advantage of their client.

Let's look at this situation, where, on a complex bankruptcy case one attorney asks an expert the following question:

"What is the value of this contract?"
"It's worth 10 million dollars."

What does worth mean? What does the expert mean when using that word? How are all 20 of the attorneys listening in on the case defining the word "worth?" How are the readers of the transcript defining the word "worth?" The expert may be implying "worth" to be contract revenues. The questioner may assume that "worth" means net profits. Others may assume "worth" is retained earnings. All of which are very different. Without a standard and mutually understood definition, much is lost and much damage will be done. We all use undefined words to promote our agenda. <u>An expert's use of important, undefined words is an indication of weakness in his/her findings.</u>

In large litigations, there could be 20 to 25 attorneys who each have their own definitions of "worth." And what would the jury and judge think? Assuming each of the 20 attorney's hourly rate is $700 (not unusual), for every hour of confusion or misinterpretation that could mean $700 X 20 attorneys X 1 hour = $14,000/hr. After awhile, you're talking real money!

And, what if that answer remains undefined. The various interests may assume their own definitions of "worth", resulting in a decision that greatly and perhaps inappropriately benefits one interest over another. That could result in millions of dollars. Or someone could go to jail because one word was left undefined.

Always use the follow up question,

- "When you used the word "xxxx," what did you mean?"
- "When you used the word "worth," what did you mean?"

or

- "When you said, 'It's worth 10 million dollars,' what did you mean?"

Never make assumptions about word meaning!

Let's look at O.J. Simpson and how he answers a question from Detective Lange that contains an undefined word, "arrested. (see 13A, page 110).

In this question, Lange asks O.J.:

"**Lange:** Were you arrested at one time for something?

Simpson: No. I mean, five years ago we had a big fight, six years ago. I don't know. I know I ended up doing community service.

Now, here, Lange assumes O.J. knows the word "arrested" like he (Lange) knows it. Assumptions are always a mistake. The word "arrest" has been debated and litigated in the courts for many, many years. The meaning of the word is defined through court decisions and many, many people misinterpret the meaning. Does Lange intend the word to be interpreted in a legal sense or a general sense? Many lay people equate "arrest" to being put in jail. An "arrest" is simply a deprivation of liberty, which does not necessarily involve incarceration. The detention could be for 2 minutes. However, there are lay people who do know that, so they may see the opportunity that the word "arrest" allows them "wiggle" and Alvin can find a way to hide in that word to create an advantage. This could all be resolved by first asking the question, "O.J., if I were to use the word "arrested," how would you define it?" Then both would have a mutual understanding of the word and the decoding process would be much more definitive.

So, contamination can flourish when words are left undefined or unanswered, resulting in unwarranted or unfounded assumptions. The truth can just lie there, undisturbed.

Chapter 10

HOW TO ASK THE RIGHT QUESTION, THE RIGHT WAY

I asked the pastor,

"May I smoke while I pray?"
Absolutely Not

"May I pray while I smoke?"
Absolutely

Here are some first questions/requests that may be properly constructed to help minimize contamination and produce uncontaminated responses:

- Tell me why you are here.
- Why am I here?
- What happened?
- What brought you here?
- Tell me about yourself.

The question structure determines the response. Structure your _initial_ questions to promote open, uncontaminated responses. Use only mutually understood words. Then look for precision, accuracy, simplicity, and directness. You then focus on where those are missing.

All of these questions/requests are open ended. They allow the subject great latitude in determining where they start.

Think about it. Where do you start? Where you start determines where you finish. Where the subject starts her response is very important. It gives you insight into how they think and how they express themselves. It can tell you if they are linear, chronological thinkers or something else. It gives you a glimpse into what you can expect and to compare later responses. In short, these early explanations, discussions, will form the foundation to analyze and interpret the subject's overall response.

How do you answer your insurance company questionnaire that asks: Do you smoke? Let's say you have an occasional cigar. Of course, you answer "No." The word "smoke" to you, the applicant, means (self-serving) something regular, an addiction, and that definition allows you to say no.

How about the question, "Do you have an issue with alcohol?" Now is the time for the applicant to self-define the word, "issue." Of course she defines it as something that is ongoing, constant, serious, habitual. And, even though she's been arrested for drunk driving, her answer "No" is quite truthful because she was, after all, only arrested once, and to her there is no pattern. She has the liberty of defining the word "issue." By allowing her that liberty, you invite The Weasel Effect (see below).

The mistake we often make as inquirers, inquisitors, investors, investigators, and parents is to allow our subject to take advantage of "wiggle" words, such as "issue," and "smoke" and to apply their own, self-serving definition of those wiggle words to their answers. We also make the mistake of making our questions too general, as when my mom asked me "Joey, what happened?" I call it the Weasel effect:

The Weasel Effect:
Subject gets you to believe one thing, while on the record saying something else.

So, my mom asked me an open-ended general wiggle question which allowed me to weasel out of telling the complete truth by telling a partial truth: "I fell on Mr. Tuinier's driveway." I led her to believe the huge, bleeding, gaping wound on my left knee was due to my fall on Mr. Tuinier's driveway. I was, and I am, a weasel.

If a parent asks their child when the child comes home 2 hours after her curfew, "Where were you?" The child then tells the parent everywhere they were except where they were that caused them to be 2 hours late. They answer the question, but they answer it partially, incompletely, and with partial truths, but usually sufficiently to wiggle out of trouble. We need to learn how to structure our questions; then learn how to interpret the response, especially the response that doesn't answer the question.

So, how should we structure our questions to get to the truth and eliminate The Weasel Effect? Here we go:

In the case of the parent who wants to know why their child is 2 hours late, a better question would be:

The original question was, "Where were you?"
A better question would be: "Why are you 2 hours late?"
More specific.
Or, a more commanding "Tell me why you are 2 hours late."
Specific and commanding. This structure adds specificity and makes it more difficult to wiggle out of the question.

My mom's question, "Joey, what happened?" could take on a more specific form:

"Joey, what caused that huge, gaping cut?" or something like that.

The question, "Do you have an issue with alcohol?" should be structured:

- "Have you within the last three years been arrested for any alcohol related issue?"
- "Have you in the last 10 years from the date of this application smoked?"

If you're an attorney, the first thing you may wish to ask your client (after you have established a standard to calibrate responses) is: "Tell me what happened." Then listen carefully. Now it's natural for a pause to this question. It's difficult to answer, and you as the attorney may not have laid a proper foundation for a candid response. Let's assume you've given them the usual spiel about it's in their best interests to be completely truthful with you, that you have an attorney-client relationship that protects such disclosures, and it's only with the complete truth that you, as thjeir attorney, can put together the appropriate defense strategy to obtain the proper disposition. Carefully absorb the subject's response and non-response taking note of the words, pauses, eye blinks, emotion, all the things we've talked about in prior chapters. Keep track of the pronouns and verbs used to help determine whether the subject is being completely truthful with you, by following the lessons I teach you in this book. I often suggest you obtain that response in their own handwriting, giving them unlined paper and as much time as they need to provide a full and complete response. Encourage them to provide details, including physical markers, conversations, identifications — in short, ask them to relive the incident and describe it all to you. Determine your legal strategy from that document. It will be invaluable to you — not just immediately, but far down that legal journey. From that document, you will be able to identify witnesses and evidence you may have never known existed.

What if you are about to purchase a business or property? That decision may depend upon the information the seller provides you. How do you go about minimizing your risk?

Let's say you're buying a business. At the first due diligence meeting you ask, "Tell me about your business." Use that opening and pay particular attention to how they start their description of the business. The first item brought up will be the portion of the business they are most proud of. The portion of the business that is never brought up will be their weakest. Pay attention to what you are told and, more importantly, to what you are not told.

How about if you are a financial analyst, evaluating a company to determine how to rate them for the market. Take a look at the target company's last two public quarterly earnings conference transcripts to analyze the chief executive's responses to analysts' questions. See my examples below. Pay particular attention to the pronoun use of the executive as she responds to the questions and see where the pronoun "I" is used. The pronoun "I" is rarely used by executives in public settings and when it is, it is an important event. A lot depends what follows the "I" and that's where experience and skill in analysis is necessary to interpret the executive's statement. The executive's frequent use of "I think" is less important than if he/she uses "I feel." "Think" is something fleeting. "Feel" has an emotional factor that requires much more thought and personal commitment. These words are important. Never underestimate their importance.

Always look for the wiggle words. If you're unable to define a word that could be a wiggle word in a written statement that you're reviewing after the fact, look earlier in the statement to see if the subject defines it sufficiently for you to know what he means. If there is nothing, force yourself not to rely upon the statement. Look for other statements/evidence to rely on.

Remember, the words used in responses are a reflection of what the subject is thinking at the time they were used. They represent a picture, not a movie. Their meaning is static, not dynamic.

- "When you say you "slipped and fell," what did you mean?"
- "What do you mean when you say, "I got caught up in traffic?"
- "What do you mean when you use the word, "hit?"

Again, your question structure determines the response. After having the subject define their words, use those words in your question to drive precision and accuracy and to eliminate "wiggle."

You need to correctly and carefully structure your questions so that you eliminate "wiggle," and force the subject to be specific. Always keep in mind that you may need to define even the most seemingly well-understood words that are "key" words. If in doubt, define. You can always ask, "What does the word, "assets," mean to you?" If you think your question(s) may be offensive, use the introduction, "I may ask you seemingly obvious questions or ask you to define the words you use. I ask them so that both of us can fully understand what we are saying to each other, so bear with me." Then ask your questions. When he uses the word, "assets," and "shape," ask him to define them or the statement, by asking, "When you said your assets were in good shape," what did you mean? I frequently use the question, "What did you mean when you said."

Chapter 11

STATEMENT EXAMPLES AND ANALYSIS

First a little lesson in first person and past tense words. Let's go to Shakespeare.

> *When I saw you I fell in love,*
> *and you smiled because you knew.*
> *—William Shakespeare*

Look at the first person pronoun "I" and the past tense verb "saw," the first person pronoun "I" and the past tense verb "fell," the second person "you," the past tense verb "smiled," and the second person "you" and finally the past tense "knew." Note the pronoun use and verb use is consistent. Does this appear to you to be from the heart, and do you find it believable? You should — this is very believable. Pronouns and verb tenses are very, very important in getting the truth.

Analysis of statements requires a series of questions. You'll be asking the question, "How else could that be stated?" Why was that word used at that time in the statement? Why did they

Simplicity is the key to getting the truth. The truthful and complete statement or response is simple, clear, precise, and direct. Anything else is suspicious.

use that word when they used a similar word earlier to describe the same feeling? What would have been the simplest way to say that? When speaking about the "gun," why do the pronouns change? Why would they say, "I picked up the gun," and then later say, "I shot the Remington?" Why does she "tell" somebody one thing, but "state" the same thing to someone else? Why doesn't she deny taking the money? How could he know what cashier's checks look like when he stated earlier he didn't? And so on.

Here is one of the statements I obtained from a young man who reported his car as stolen. The question starting off this statement was, "Tell me what happened."

I came home around 10:00pm in the evening. I parked the car in our driveway. The doors were locked and the alarm was activated. I went to bed about 11:00pm. When I came out at 7:00AM in the morning I discovered that the car was gone and a part of the driver side window was still on the ground, broken out. A police report was filed immediately at the local precinct.

11A:

In this case, we need look no further than the first paragraph. When someone is recounting a past incident, the first thing we expect in a truthful response is a simple and direct statement. Further, we look for first person singular pronouns, past tense verbs, all in the active voice. The active voice is a statement where the actor commits the act. "I threw the ball," is the active voice. The active voice creates a simple, efficient, and direct statement. The active voice is used in the best denial, "I didn't do it." The other voice at the end of this first paragraph is the passive voice. We want to note where the voice changes, in this case from the active voice (which was used in the first two sentences) to the passive voice. Changes in voice are important and may be indicative of deception. "The ball was thrown by...." is the passive voice because we don't know the actor.

For example, his sentence "I (first person singular) <u>came</u> (past tense verb) home around 10:00 PM in the evening," is a well-structured and truthful sentence in the active voice. I can rely on it because the writer committed to it by using the first person singular pronoun "I" and by using the past tense verb "came" in a simple and direct response. Commitment is extremely important in truth-getting. Alvin doesn't allow commitment if it is a lie. A lack of commitment by not using the "I" or by using the passive voice are tracks to lead you to partial truths.

The "...in the evening," needs to be noted. It is unnecessary and redundant. Unnecessary and redundant words (descriptions) are what I call "artillery" (to be explained in depth later) which is used by persons who want you to believe they're telling the truth when they're not. Artillery, in short, is a strategy designed to entice you into listening to the words, phrases, movements, nuances, volume, emotions, etc., — instead of the message. This is not necessarily significant, but it needs to be noted.

The next sentence is the flag waver. "I parked the car in our driveway." There is a first person singular pronoun "<u>I</u>," a past tense verb "<u>parked</u> the car in our driveway." Now, I believe this sentence is also truthful. It also is in the active voice. The problem is in the missing possessive pronoun next to "car." We know he is capable of using possessive pronouns because he possesses his driveway with an "our driveway." But he (Alvin) didn't state, "I parked <u>my</u> car in our driveway." Why not? This was his opportunity to eliminate all other cars that he parked in his driveway, but he chose (important to remember, *chose*) not to use the possessive pronoun.

Also, now he changes his voice to the passive voice in the next statement, " The doors were locked and the alarm was activated." A change in voice, particularly when one shows the active voice, is a sign of deception. The first two sentences are in the active voice, followed abruptly by the passive voice. Alvin forced this change in voice. You can tell a partial truth if you don't commit to it. The statement doesn't say who, when, or where the "doors were locked and the alarm was activated." Passive voice allows a statement without commitment.

These are all tracks. I know the subject is being deceptive. My interrogation reveals the truth. He was behind on his car payments. He drove his car down a lonely road, set it on fire, broke out one of the windows and pocketed the broken glass. Left the scene driving his buddy's car who followed him to the scene, parked his buddy's car in "our" driveway, sprinkled the glass on the driveway, and made the false stolen car report and claim in the morning. He told the truth in his statement. The tracks were the missing pronoun "my" or "our" in the second sentence and the change in voice in the third sentence. He was later charged with filing a false police report.

11B:

This young employee deposited a no-account check for $1,500 into her personal checking account.

A no-account check is a check that no longer has an underlying valid account. Let's say you moved from Florida to Michigan and closed your Florida bank account. You neglected to destroy all your old, now invalid, checks. Then, someone writes a check on your old closed account. That would be a no-account check.

If she knew the check was a no-account check, the minimum punishment would be employment termination. If she didn't know the check was a no-account check, there would be no need for discipline or punishment.

Q. Tell me what happened?

A.

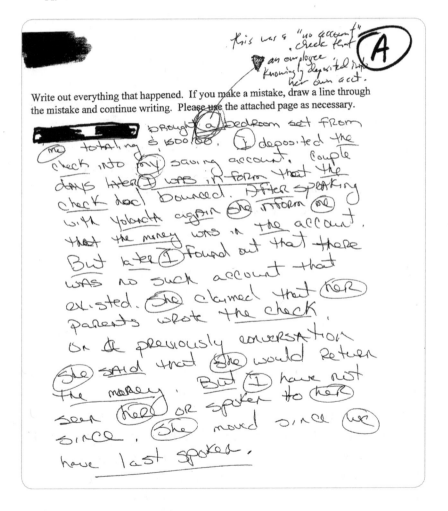

In this statement, I calibrate to the individual to help fully understand what I'm being given. I see she is able to use the possessive pronoun "my" when stating, "I deposited the check in my saving account." So, I know she can use the pronoun "my." But "my" is missing when she refers to her bedroom set. That's curious. But it's understandable if the bedroom set she refers to is one of several bedroom sets she had. Maybe her aunt gave her a bedroom set and she stored the bedroom set in her garage until she sold it. In that case, she wouldn't have had a personal attachment to that bedroom set and the missing "my" would be understandable. So, I ask her the question, "Tell me about your bedroom set." She advised she and her husband used that bedroom set for 10 years. Did you use it everyday? "Yes, we used it everyday for our clothes and bedroom items." Now I know she is being deceptive. These are not idle mistakes. The track was the non-use of a possessive pronoun when there is personal, emotional, and psychological attachment. That knowledge leads to a confession. She stated she needed the money and hoped it would go undetected and not reported. She was terminated.

11C:

"He lunged at me right about the time the gun went off."

— Jodi Arias 3/6/13

Well, by now you should know my response. "He lunged at me" is probably true. It's the " . . . right about the time the gun went off" that takes a leap. More believable statements would read something like, "I shot him when he lunged at me," or "He lunged at me and I shot him," or a weaker "He lunged at me and the gun went off." But she didn't say that, did she? A statement that is vague, uncertain, and noncommittal is not reliable.

11D:

""I, in 10 years in his power there, never asked
Tony Blair for any favors and never received
any," Murdoch said in April, pounding his hand
on the table for emphasis."
    — Rupert Murdoch, CNN, Monday May 28, 2012.

I'm sorry, but did he have people working for him? Could it be that he is being truthful by stating very specifically that "I . . . never asked Tony Blair . . . ?" However, the fact may be that he told one of his trusted employees to make the offer. So, read statements very carefully to see what isn't said, even more than what is said. Had he said, "I, nor any of my employees or agents, in 10 years in my power there, never asked Tony Blair for any favors and never received any." That would be a much more impactful, more convincing, and more revealing statement. Since his statement wasn't structured that way, we can only conclude that he couldn't state that.

11E:

Aired December 2, 2012 - 16:00 ET CNN
Martin Savidge interview of John McAfee

SAVIDGE: He used that 'sir' a lot. His hair is
jet black, part of his disguise and he asked
us to wait for his hair to dry before starting
our interview. And that interview ranged from
completely convincing like when I asked about his
neighbor's murder. Did you kill Gregory Faull?

MCAFFEE: I barely knew the man and why would I
kill him? He was a neighbor that lived 200 yards
down the beach.

How is that a convincing response? He never denied killing his neighbor!

11F:

> I am an honest person. I would never, will never get a penny from anybody that does not belong to me. This is totally against my principals and my family principles. I don't take cash even from my husbands wallet without telling him. This is totally a nonsense situation. Everybody who knows me know I am a reliable and honest person.

This is a written statement from a woman who was one of 8 suspects in the theft of money. I want you to focus on what she didn't say, not what she said. Did she deny taking the money? No! When someone has an opportunity to deny an act they didn't do and doesn't, they probably did it.

11G:

"I've suspected that my husband has been fooling around but when confronted with the evidence, he denied everything and said it would never happen again."

Never stop listening.

11H:

Question Structure for Depositions
Here are some facts to consider for this exercise. A will was signed, witnessed and executed. Later, another will, believed to be ill-

conceived and fraudulent, was signed by the testator when the testator was believed mentally incompetent, witnessed by two persons, and executed by *Mr. Recipient* following the testator's death. These questions are prepared for the deposition of the *witnesses* in the second will.

Jim Miller is the testator in this sequence.
Mr. Recipient is the new, main benefactor in the new will.

Precision is the nemesis of deception. Promote verbosity and volume using mutually understood words, but look for simplicity and precision to get the truth.

Untruthful people hide in hard-to-define *wiggle* words that are vague, unresponsive, and difficult to confirm. A truthful response will be clear, direct, and precise. The truthful person wants the truth to be seen and heard. An untruthful person wants to obfuscate or conceal the truth.

Once you've asked your simple, open-ended questions using mutually defined words to promote volume and verbosity, you'll need to zero in on the subject's wiggle words. By forcing precision, you will force the truth to surface. The following questions are designed to promote precision. The words in the questions are as important as the words in their respective responses.

The below sequence may seem laborious. It is. But it is necessary to follow to make sure you build on mutually known words. Your case will be much stronger if your foundation is sound.

As you listen to the responses, force the deposed to define their "wiggle" words with the question, "What did you mean when you said, 'I talked to him the other day'?" Force him to define "talk." Was it in person, by phone, by text? Force the deposed to define words until you are comfortable there is little or no "wiggle" when it's used. The more precise the details, the more likely you will be able to corroborate or disprove the response. You will greatly enhance your understanding of what the subject is saying, and the subject will find much less room to maneuver when answering difficult questions. It puts much more pressure on the subject when he/she knows there is no room for error. This approach will train the deposed to answer questions more precisely and accurately. So, at the cost of time in the beginning, you save much time at the end. And, more importantly, the deposed won't be able to escape the truth-getting that's about to occur.

Now, we have to be reasonable in this process. You can't possibly define every word. The following is an example of how I would structure a session. Once you go through the process, it becomes easier and more enlightening. Further, the deposed learns that he/she cannot use a word that is vague because you will challenge them and force them to define the word. That will put more pressure on them, will force them to be more precise, and will make it much more difficult for them to be deceptive.

Following the introductions and legal discussions, start with the following sequence (assuming the subject knows the purpose of the deposition):

1. *Please tell me what happened.* (The subject responds that he first met Jim Miller in 1992, among other things.)
2. *Give me more when you say, "first met Jim Miller in 1992."* Listen carefully to how he defines those words. If his understanding is not clear or has wiggle words within it, then you must push him/her further to fully define the words to eliminate any future confusion. Following that discussion wherein the meaning of the words is discussed and the parties agree to a mutual understanding, then proceed with the question. One might argue that you are helping prepare the subject for the subsequent question.

The meaning of the words trumps any benefit you would gain from surprise.

3. If I ask, "Were you together with someone," what would the word, "together" mean?

4. How many times were you together with Jim Miller?

5. Where were you together with Jim Miller?

6. If I ask the question, "Who was present," what would that mean to you?

7. Who was present when you were together with Jim Miller?

8. When did you first meet Mr. Recipient?

9. If I use the phrase, "witness the will," what does "witness the will" mean to you?

10. Why were you a witness to the will?

11. When did Mr. Recipient first ask you to witness the will?
    By now, most of the key words and phrases are mutually understood and I'll leave the remainder of these questions for you to identify which words to define in a question. It's a good practice to not ask the "word meaning" questions in the same way. Keep the pressure on the deposed, by mixing up the way you ask the questions. Remember, you need clarity and mutual understanding when asking questions and interpreting responses.

12. Where were you when Mr. Recipient first asked you to witness the will?

13. Who was present when he first asked you to witness the will?

14. What did he say when he first asked you to witness the will?

15. How did he say it?

16. When did you next talk to anyone about witnessing the will?

17. What did Mr. Recipient promise you to witness the will?

18. Did anyone else make a promise to you to witness the will?

19. Why would you agree to witness the will?

20. Do you have anything written down regarding your witnessing the will?
21. Where did the witnessing take place?
22. Describe where the witnessing took place.
23. How did you get to the place where the will was witnessed?
24. Who was present when you witnessed the will?
25. When did the witnessing take place?
26. Did you have any conversations with anyone after you witnessed this will?
27. If I use the word, "observe," what does "observe" mean to you?
28. What did you observe at the witnessing?
29. Is that your signature on the will?
30. What does your signature on the will mean?
31. Did you see Jim Miller read that will?
32. Did you see Jim Miller sign that will?
33. Describe what you saw when you saw Jim Miller read that will.
34. Please describe in detail what you saw.
35. Did he say anything?
36. Did you say anything?
37. Did Mr. Recipient say anything?
38. How did he sign that will?
39. Who was present when he signed that will?
40. What happened after you signed that will?
41. Where did you go after signing that will?
42. Describe what you did the day you witnessed the will from the time you woke up until the time you went to bed.
43. If I use the word, "ever," in a question, what does that mean?
44. Please list all people you have ever talked to about the witnessing of this will.
45. Is Mr. Recipient, or anyone else, paying you for expenses concerning your appearance here today?

46. If I use the word, "communicate," what does, "communicate," mean to you?

47. How do you communicate with Mr. Recipient?

48. *What phone(s) do you use to call Mr. Recipient?*

49. What phone number do you use to call Mr. Recipient?

50. What is/are the phones and/or phone numbers you use to call Mr. Recipient?

51. If I use the phrase, "anything of value," — what would that mean to you?

52. Have you received anything of value from Mr. Recipient?

53. Did Mr. Recipient offer you anything of value?

54. If I use the term, "anyone," what does that mean to you?

55. Do you expect anything of value from anyone for witnessing this will?

56. Do any of your family members expect anything of value for your witnessing this will?

57. If I use the phrase, "contingent upon," what does that mean to you?

58. If I use the word, "disposition," what does that mean to you?

59. Do you expect anything of value contingent upon the disposition of this will?

60. Do any of your family members expect anything of value contingent upon the disposition of this will?

And so on . . .

The key is to make sure you always know exactly what the deposed is saying, and, just as important, you know he knows what you are asking.

(CNN) — "I do not use crack cocaine, nor am I an addict of crack cocaine."

— Toronto Mayor Rob Ford 5/23/13

He used present tense (I do not use) and the word "addict" has wiggle room. Also, a simpler more direct statement would have been, "I never used crack cocaine." Look for simplicity, directness, and clarity.

Chapter 12

INVESTMENTS

Would you like to have an edge on others when making investment decisions? Of course you would. In addition to using fundamental analysis, technical analysis, Fibonacci analysis, use this truth-getting analysis. See how this analysis can help you get that edge.

12A
ORACLE'S 1Q 2011
9/16/10

Let's take a look at Oracle's (ORCL) quarter 2011 earnings call, September 16, 2010, from www. seekingalpha.com. Specifically, we'll focus on the comments by President Safra Catz regarding the guidance for 2Q. If you need to know the truth, why not look to the person who should be most informed. Here is the transcript from Seeking Alpha:

Truth-getting is more about discovering partial truths than uncovering lies. A partial truth that is misleading is a lie – let's make no mistake. But it's much easier and more productive to get the whole truth by calling a lie a partial truth. The key to truth-getting is to look through the eyes of the prevaricator, not the investigator.

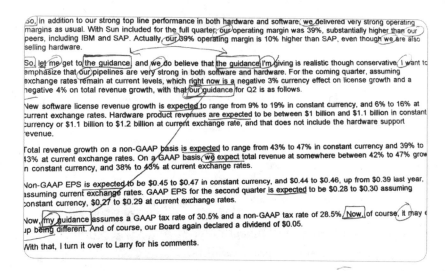

So, in addition to our strong top line performance in both hardware and software, we delivered very strong operating margins as usual. With Sun included for the full quarter, our operating margin was 39%, substantially higher than our peers, including IBM and SAP. Actually, our 39% operating margin is 10% higher than SAP, even though we are also selling hardware.

So, let me get to the guidance, and we do believe that the guidance I'm giving is realistic though conservative. I want to emphasize that our pipelines are very strong in both software and hardware. For the coming quarter, assuming exchange rates remain at current levels, which right now is a negative 3% currency effect on license growth and a negative 4% on total revenue growth, with that our guidance for Q2 is as follows.

New software license revenue growth is expected to range from 9% to 19% in constant currency, and 6% to 16% at current exchange rates. Hardware product revenues are expected to be between $1 billion and $1.1 billion in constant currency or $1.1 billion to $1.2 billion at current exchange rate, and that does not include the hardware support revenue.

Total revenue growth on a non-GAAP basis is expected to range from 43% to 47% in constant currency and 39% to 43% at current exchange rates. On a GAAP basis, we expect total revenue at somewhere between 42% to 47% grow in constant currency, and 38% to 43% at current exchange rates.

Non-GAAP EPS is expected to be $0.45 to $0.47 in constant currency, and $0.44 to $0.46, up from $0.39 last year, assuming current exchange rates. GAAP EPS for the second quarter is expected to be $0.28 to $0.30 assuming constant currency, $0.27 to $0.29 at current exchange rates.

Now, my guidance assumes a GAAP tax rate of 30.5% and a non-GAAP tax rate of 28.5%. Now, of course, it may e up being different. And of course, our Board again declared a dividend of $0.05.

With that, I turn it over to Larry for his comments.

See how President Catz refers to her corporate guidance. My markings in the 2nd paragraph show her first referring to this guidance as "the guidance," then "the guidance," then "our guidance," and finally in the sixth[th] paragraph, "my guidance." These are significant changes that have to be explained by the giver of the statement. If no explanation is provided, then we must assume the literal meaning. "The guidance" shows no commitment. "Our guidance" reflects some commitment. "My guidance" shows full commitment.

Further, notice she introduces her guidance statement in the third[rd] paragraph with "the guidance I'm giving." When anyone begins a statement with "I'm giving" or "I can tell you this" or "This is what I can share with you," etc., you cannot rely on what follows, even though there is the "I" pronoun. See Chapter 6 on introductions. You can't rely on it because the person stating it is not committing to it. They are qualifying their statement. They're simply, "giving it." Thus, they are not committing to what they subsequently state.

So, we cannot rely on what Ms. Catz tells us until the sixth[th] paragraph sentence where she now commits to providing "my guidance" and there is no "I'm giving" that prefaces it. She doesn't say "this guidance" or "the guidance I gave" which could be construed to be a summation. She differentiates this sentence by calling it "my guidance" and that is entirely different and now very personal. Now, and only now, can we rely on what she tells us in this sentence: "my guidance assumes a GAAP tax rate of 30.5% and a non-GAAP rate of 28.5%." In short, we rely most on what the speaker commits to.

Based on this analysis and Ms. Catz's prior remarks (see below), I opine that Ms. Catz is <u>much</u> more ebullient in her own guidance than the corporate guidance she gave. As an investor, I'd like to know that a chief executive is more enthusiastic about corporate guidance than the guidance she is actually providing. Note the last bullet: "…I'm giving is realistic though conservative." She shows she believes that through her pronouns.

(From http://seekingalpha.com ORCL Q1 2011 Earnings Call Transcript, underline & *italics* my edit):

- "So, in addition to our <u>*strong top line*</u> performance in both hardware and software, we <u>delivered *very strong*</u> operating margins as usual. With Sun included for the full quarter; our operating margin was 39%, *substantially higher* than our peers, including IBM and SAP. Actually, our 39% operating margin is <u>*10% higher*</u> than SAP, *even though* we are also selling hardware."
- "So, let me get to the guidance, and we do believe that the guidance I'm giving is realistic though <u>*conservative*</u>."

12B
APPLE'S EARNINGS CONFERENCES
F1Q 2013 ON 1/23/13 AND F2Q 2013
ON 4/23/13

The Corporate Use of "We" pronoun:

The use of "we" in the corporate world needs discussion. The pronoun "we" is culturally expected and encouraged in the corporate setting. The "we" builds teamwork and allows the user to share reward and benefit. It also allows the user to share blame, responsibility, and accountability. You can hide in the "we." So, many executives overuse the "we" in their commentary, mostly to build a better corporate environment and, sometimes, to hide. To some extent, the value of analyzing the "we" in corporate statements is weakened.

We need to note that the use of the pronoun "I" in such statements, therefore, takes on special importance. With the corporate emphasis on the "we," when an executive uses the "I," we need to pay even more attention to the all important "I."

The opening executive statements for publically held company quarterly conferences (like AAPL's F1Q 2013 and F2Q 2013 below) are usually written by a team of people and not necessarily by the executive. So, analysis of that opening statement needs to include the knowledge, that even though the executive is giving the statement, the executive's own words are not necessarily being used. However, the executive is still giving that statement in his/her own voice. I feel we can still find the opening statement useful since the executive is still giving his/her stamp of approval on those words and adding their own unique nuances to the way that statement is given.

Let's compare Apple's Tim Cook's opening statements for the F1Q and F2Q 2013.

F1Q 2013: "Thanks, Nancy and good afternoon everyone and thank you for joining us. We are incredibly pleased to report an extraordinary quarter with $54.5 billion in revenue and new records for iPhone and the iPad sales. No technology company has ever reported these kinds of results."

F2Q 2013: "Thanks, Nancy. Hello, everyone and thank you for joining us. We have a lot of news to share with you today about the details of our March quarter as well as a significant increase to our capital return program."

Now, which statement gives a better outlook? We don't need statement analysis or extensive analysis of any kind to see there was greater enthusiasm, greater expectations, and greater excitement in the F1Q. The words *"incredibly pleased," "extraordinary," "new records," "has ever,"* and *"these kinds of results,"* tell the story.

In the F2Q, those superlatives are missing. We have no need to read the fine details to know the outlook for APPL in F3Q is not good. And it wasn't, as the following shows (source Google Finance on 12/15/2013):

AAPL Stock price at 4/23/2013 (date of F2Q 2013 earnings report): $406.13
AAPL Stock price at 6/28/2013 (end of F2Q 2013): $396.53

Further, my analysis of the two quarterly earnings call statements and Tim Cook's responses to analysts' questions revealed the following:

Snapshot of Tim Cook's thinking at Earnings Conferences:

From F1Q 2013 1/23/2013

- He is concerned about iPhone demand.
- Concerned about Mac demand.
- Bullish on iMaps and online services (iTunes, etc.).
- Bullish on China.
- Neutral on Apple TV.
- Sees cannibalization as huge opportunity.

From F2Q 2013 4/23/2013

- Lots of obtuse and difficult explanations = uncertainty; defensive.
- Weakening belief in China.
- Future growth is a concern.
- Bullish on tablets.
- Unsure about screen size on iPhone 5.

A sample from Seeking Alpha for APPL's F1Q 2013:

Ben Reitzes - Barclays

Okay, thanks a lot Tim. And then just my follow-up is with regard to web services, online services, there has been a lot of publicity around maps and can you give us an update there? And then looking forward how does the year look in terms of innovation, in terms of iOS 7 and your online and web services, how will that drive Apple?

Tim Cook

Well, let me start with the second part of this. We are working on some incredible stuff. The pipeline is chock-full, I don't want to comment about a specific product, but we feel great about what we have got in store. In terms of Maps, we have made a number of improvements to Maps since the introduction of iOS 6 back in September and will roll out even more improvements across the rest of the year and we are going to keep working on this as I have said before until it lives up to our incredibly high standards. Users can already see many of these improvements because they include things like improved satellite and improved imaginary and improved categorization, improved local information for 1000s of businesses and so forth. The usage in maps is significantly higher than it was prior to iOS 6. In terms of other services we feel fantastic about how we're doing, in notification center we've sent over 4 trillion notifications and this is mind blowing. As Peter mentioned in his opening comment for iMessage we've sent over 450 billion and are currently sending those 6 billion per day. We've gained center, we have got over 200 million registered users, we've 800,000 apps on the App Store with over 40 billion downloads and so I feel really, really great about it, there is obviously more stuff we can do and you can bet we're thinking about all of it.

When I conduct an analysis, you will notice I circle all the pronouns and all those words or letters that act like pronouns. Pronouns are extremely important to help get the truth. I also like contraction use (as noted in Chapter 8), so I circle those as well.

In the last sentence, you see a rare "I." The personal pronoun "I" is extremely important in that when used, the speaker is declaring a personal commitment to what follows. Executives rarely use the "I" and often use the "We" because they wish to share the praise (and blame) and infer and encourage teamwork in their organizations. Tim Cook is no exception. So, when he uses an "I" it is very important. ". . . and so I feel really, really great about it . . ." An "I feel" is much stronger than an "I think." "Feel" has a deeper, more emotional attachment than "I think." Further, he uses the "I think" very often and only rarely uses the "I feel." Again, we must calibrate to the subject whose statements we're analyzing. This shows he can commit. This is especially important because he rarely uses the personal pronoun "I," so when he does it is doubly important. The "it" he refers to is iMaps — you can make the connection if you closely read the question and Cook's response. It's through that analysis that I conclude, as noted above for F1Q 2013's conference analysis, that Cook is bullish on iMaps.

A Tim Cook response sample from Seeking Alpha for AAPL's F2Q 2013:

However, I take your point is that market did grow by 30%, we still, after that normalization, we grew less than that. And so I think the question or the - this point is not lost and we do want to grow faster. We don't view it, however, as the only measure of our health. The things that are very important to us in addition to market share and unit volumes include things like customer sat, which were the highest by far winning J.D. Power's nine times consecutively and the customer loyalty and repurchase rates, which were the highest by far the 95% according to Kantar. And the ecosystem commerce, which attracts developers is incredible analysis says that we have 74%, so basically $3 out of $4 that are spent on - apps are spent in our ecosystem.

And if you then looked at usage statistics, they are staggering at the usage of iOS versus other operating systems. And so market shares are important and unit volumes are important, but these other things for us are extremely important, because we are all about customer experience and enriching lives.

This section in F2Q 2013 shows Cook's difficulty in responding to AAPL's relevant lack of growth, in fact he admits he is disappointed, and later attempts to deflect the response to areas where he cites where AAPL is doing well. We look for simple, direct responses. Anything else is suspicious and indicative of sensitivity and weakness.

So, you can see how powerful this analysis can be to help you understand the true messages of executives at earnings conferences and to enhance your investment decisions.

Chapter 13

EXERCISES

13A
THE O.J. SIMPSON INTERVIEW

This exercise will give you a better understanding of how to ask questions and how to interpret responses to those questions. Please don't interpret any of my analysis as a criticism of the work of Los Angeles Police Department Detectives Tom Lange and Phillip Vannatter.

I committed many of the same errors before I learned the art of properly constructing questions and setting up the interview so as to minimize contamination and get the truth. So, this is, in no way, meant to be a criticism of their work. It's a review that's necessary for all of us to grow.

First let me point out a couple of general observations.

The best thinking is to have one interviewer and one interviewee. One-to-one interviews help control contamination and maintain continuity. When Lange and Vannatter asked their questions, each one had their own agenda. Each communicated in different and supplemental ways. For example, each officer reacted to Simpson's responses. Each one may have reacted to his partner's question. A facial expression, notes taken, a sideways glance, a raised eyebrow, a curling of the lips, a wrinkling of the forehead all contaminate what may follow. We need to minimize all these communication variables to minimize contamination.

Each interviewer has his own agenda and line of questioning. You'll see in this transcript where one officer will ask a question and before that line of questioning is completed, the other officer will ask a different question, making the query non-linear, resulting in tangential and incomplete information. In linear questioning, the interviewer asks a question, listens to the response, then develops and pursues that response to provide more details. In a non-linear strategy, the interviewer asks a question, and then asks another question not related to the first question or the first question's response. The non-linear line of questioning allows a guilty person to avoid providing the details the investigators need to help determine the facts to support the suspect's guilt (or innocence). The need in this interview was to gather facts that may or may not implicate Simpson to the murders. So, a linear strategy is needed here.

Now, there may be a time when a non-linear strategy is desirable. I might use that approach if I'm interviewing a very calculating suspect to help elicit factual incriminating statements that he/she just blurts out — statements that only the person responsible would know. For example, let's say we're interviewing a man who is suspected of killing a young lady. The young lady was murdered in a very peculiar way (she was strangled, then shot after she was dead), and only the one responsible for that killing would know. I may ask a suspect a series of non-threatening questions: What is your full name? Where do you live? How long have you lived there? And, then I may quickly insert a threatening question, like, "How was Melanie killed?" to see how the subject responded. That would be a non-linear strategy.

While these introductory questions are essential in calibrating to the subject, as discussed earlier, you always have to be ready. I broke one of my cases because of the subject's response during this introductory phase. This subject was the manager in charge of vendor contracts. I asked the subject the usual questions, full name, date of birth, where he lived, etc. He struggled to answer the question, "Where do you live?" Now, that's not a hard question.

So following the regular interview, which yielded little, I noted that struggle and conducted some extensive follow up. The investigation showed the manager recently moved into an apartment that was surreptitiously owned by a vendor. The vendor was recently awarded an extended contract. That knowledge was the key to an admission in a subsequent interview with the manager, which eventually led to his firing. So, as an investigator you need to always be alert and always be in the absorption mode. You just never know.

Use the following discussion to help you set the table so that you have a greater likelihood to obtain the truth (which may be deception).

Now, for my analysis of the June 13, 1994, Interview of O.J. Simpson by LAPD Detectives Thomas Lange and Philip Vannatter regarding the June 12, 1994, murders of O.J. Simpson's wife, Nicole Simpson, and Ronald Goldman. Read this analysis line by line. There is much to learn here, and the analysis brings together many of the concepts I've covered in earlier chapters. This will provide you with great insight into how to analyze statements and find the truth. Keep in mind, we need to look at each and every word used, not only in the question, but also in the response. Even absence of words is important. Look at everything.

Vannatter: . . . my partner, Detective Lange, and we're in an interview room in Parker Center. The date is June 13th, 1994, and the time is 13:35 hours. And we're here with O.J. Simpson. Is that Orenthal James Simpson?

Simpson: Orenthal James Simpson

Use these introductory questions to help determine the subject's speaking rhythm, breathing patterns, speech nuances, eye blinking, facial expressions, speed of response, etc.

Vannatter: And what is your birthdate, Mr. Simpson?

Simpson: July 9th, 1947.

Vannatter: OK. Prior to us talking to you, as we agreed with your attorney, I'm going to give you your constitutional rights. And I would like you to listen carefully. If you don't understand anything, tell me, OK?

Simpson: All right.

Vannatter: OK. Mr. Simpson, you have the right to remain silent. If you give up the right to remain silent, anything you say can and will be used against you in a court of law. You have the right to speak to an attorney and to have an attorney present during the questioning. If you so desire and cannot afford one, an attorney will be appointed for you without charge before questioning. Do you understand your rights?

Simpson: Yes, I do.

Note this is not a simple yes, it's "Yes, I do."

Vannatter: Are there any questions about that?

Simpson: (unintelligible).

Vannatter: OK, you've got to speak up louder than that . . .

Simpson: OK, no.

Vannatter: OK, do you wish to give up your right to remain silent and talk to us?

Simpson: Ah, yes.

Not a simple, "yes."

Vannatter: QK, and you give up your right to have an attorney present while we talk?

Simpson: Mmm hmm. Yes.

Again, not a simple yes. Let's pay particular attention to simple "Yes's." Those will be special, if we see any.

Vannatter: OK. All right, what we're gonna do is, we want to . . . We're investigating, obviously, the death of your ex-wife and another man.

Lange: Someone told us that.

Who is someone? Who is us? What is that? This is the first question from Lange. The best set up for an interview (or interrogation) is one-on-one. One officer questions the subject. Or one HR representative questions the prospective employee. When you have two asking questions, you no longer have a linear process. The second officer has his own set of questions, his own way of understanding responses. With two officers, the questioning process becomes tangential, not linear, and both officers will lose focus. That offers the subject a decided advantage. He can play one officer off against the other using wiggle words and indirect answers.

The person asking the questions should learn more about the subject than the subject learns about the questioner. Questions need to be short, using clearly defined words, and the questioner needs to minimize other contamination sources like facial expressions, taking notes at certain points, raising an eyebrow to one response and not another, and so on. Two questioners more than double the contamination potential. That contamination will reduce or eliminate an effective session.

Vannatter: Yeah, and we're going to need to talk to you about that. Are you divorced from her now?

"That" is undefined right now. May lead to confusion and creates 'wiggle' room for subject to take advantage of later.

Simpson: Yes.

Now a simple, 'yes.' Let's remember this one. Why now and not the other times?

Vannatter: How long have you been divorced?

Simpson: Officially? Probably close to two years, but we've been apart for a little over two years.

Are there "unofficial" divorces? Please note the first use of a contraction, "we've." This is a stressful interview. When we see the use of a contraction it is an indication of less stress. So answers with contractions tend to be answers the subject is comfortable answering. When people lie, they are under more stress. They are under less stress when telling a simple truth. In this case, he stated, "but we've been apart for a little over two years." He's very comfortable saying that so we can probably rely on that.

This also shows us he is capable of using contractions. This will be important later.

Vannatter: Have you?

Simpson: Yeah.

Note it was "yeah," not "yes."

Vannatter: What was your relationship with her? What was the . . .

Vannatter was about to ask another question, or a compound question. We need to ask simple, direct questions, and wait for the response. Good question, by the way — "What was your relationship with her?" Note the question is past tense.

Simpson: Well, we tried to get back together, and it just didn't work. It wasn't working, and so we were going our separate ways.

We cannot assume the "it" he refers to is Vannatter's "relationship." If you assume he did, that would be a mistake.

Never assume. We need to ask the subject, "When you say, 'it just didn't work,' what do you mean?"

The subject again uses a contraction in his response, "and it just didn't work." However, we can't rely on anything here until we know what "it" is.

Vannatter: Recently you tried to get back together?

Simpson: We tried to get back together for about a year, you know, where we started dating each other and seeing each other. She came back and wanted us to get back together, and . . .

Need to allow subject to completely answer the question. Now, we wonder what he was about to say.

Vannatter: Within the last year, you're talking about?

Simpson: She came back about a year and four months ago about us trying to get back together, and we gave it a shot. We gave it a shot the better part of a year. And I think we both knew it wasn't working, and probably three weeks ago or so, we said it just wasn't working, and we went our separate ways.

Note all the "we's" and "us'" in this answer. This is an indication of togetherness, showing joint agreement, and comfort in the decisions — at that time. He is talking past tense. If we believe O.J. is the killer, this answer tells me we need to look at what has happened since these decisions were made. Therein lies the reason, motive, and his rationalization for the killings.

Vannatter: OK, the two children are yours?

Simpson: Yes.

Again, a simple "yes." He has no difficulty responding with a "yes." We, therefore note when he responds with something other than a "yes." Even a "ah, yes," is different and therefore noteworthy.

Lange: She have custody?

Simpson: We have joint custody.

Lange: Through the courts?

Simpson: We went through the courts and everything. Everything is done. We have no problems with the kids, we do everything together, you know, with the kids.

Note the present tense in this answer. But also note, "we do everything together, you know, with the kids" — the qualifier is "with the kids."

Vannatter: How was your separation? What that a . . .?

Simpson: The first separation?

Vannatter: Yeah, was there problems with that?

Simpson: For me, it was big problems. I loved her, I didn't want us to separate.

Now back to past tense.

Vannatter: Uh huh. I understand she had made a couple of crime . . . crime reports or something?

Simpson: Ah, we have (sic) a big fight about six years ago on New Year's, you know, she made a report. I didn't make a report. And then we had an altercation about a year ago maybe. It wasn't a physical argument. I kicked her door or something.

Vannatter introduces the word "report" without defining it. I would prefer to define it first in my question by first asking, "If I use the term 'crime report' what would that mean to you?" Make sure both you and the subject know what every word means in the question. O.J.'s first response is "Ah," which is notable. It reveals a direct response is not coming. The question was, "she made a couple of crime . . . crime reports or something?" His response should have been, "Yes," with an explanation. Then O.J. states, "I didn't make a report." That is not what Vannatter asked — therefore, it is extra special. Unresponsive answers are notable.

Vannatter: And she made a police report on those two occasions?

Simpson: Mmm hmm. And I stayed right there until the police came, talked to them.

Again, not a "yes." And a curious response, "And I stayed right there until the police came. . ." Why did he say that? We not only look at what was said, but also what wasn't said. This comment is out of context. When something is volunteered and out of context it is doubly important. Perhaps his motive is to co-opt Lange and Vannatter to help improve his credibility.

Lange: Were you arrested at one time for something?

Simpson: No. I mean, five years ago we had a big fight, six years ago. I don't know. I know I ended up doing community service.

Not a "yes," but he did community service. That's a yes without him saying it, but the fact he didn't say "yes" is important. A response without a yes may be deniable. The contraction, "I don't know" means he probably doesn't know what the word "arrest" means — thus the wiggle answer. The contraction tells me he's comfortable answering questions without really knowing what's being asked. He's used to providing vague responses. He may have an elementary understanding of what "arrest" means and is using his non-legal status to provide a non-definitive answer. That can be corrected by making sure the word "arrest" is defined in the question or if Lange then asks O.J., "Tell me what you think the word 'arrested' means."

Vannatter: So you weren't arrested?

Simpson: No, I was never really arrested.

O.J. still is not sure what "arrest" means or he does and he's intentionally misleading Vannatter. He, like many laypersons, might think "arrest" means going to jail. Since he didn't go to jail, he thinks he wasn't arrested. One can be "arrested" without going to jail. Or, he may wish us to believe he means that — without definition we will never know.

Lange: They never booked you or . . .

Simpson: No.

A good simple answer, "No."

Vannatter: Can I ask you, when's the last time you've slept?

A questioner should never ask permission to ask a question. The questioner releases some control over the situation when doing so. And, what does the word, "slept" mean? We all think we know what it means, but we don't. "Slept" to me means the instant I lose consciousness. To others, it means when they go to bed. To others, it means when they start drifting off but are still conscious. And so on.

Simpson: I got a couple of hours sleep last night. I mean, you know, I slept a little on the plane, not much, and when I got to the hotel I was asleep a few hours when the phone call came.

Lange: Did Nicole have a housemaid that lived there?

Simpson: I believe so, yes.

Again, not a simple "yes."

Lange: Do you know her name at all?

Simpson: Evia, Elvia, something like that.

Vannatter: We didn't see her there. Did she have the day off perhaps?

Simpson: I don't know. I don't know what schedule she's on.

Interesting answer. What day are we talking about? Vannatter may be referring to when he (Vannatter) was there, O.J. may have been talking about a different day. This is worth pursuing.

Lange: Phil, what do you think? We can maybe just recount last night . . .

Vannatter: Yeah. When was the last time you saw Nicole?

"Last," is an excellent word and "the last" requires a precise response. There is only one "last" time. How would the killer answer this? It's a live torpedo in the water.

This is a critical question, and it's asked well into the O.J. interview. As part of our interview/deposition/trial strategy we must construct our critical questions and place them in the interview at strategic locations. I like the location of this critical question. It allows for calibration (see Chapter 3). Preliminary questions set the stage for well-founded analysis of responses to critical questions.

Critical questions must be structured simply, precisely, and carefully. I would have liked this critical question to read, "When did you last see Nicole?" That question uses fewer words (6 instead of 8) and is slimmer, sharper, and more compact. It carries more of a punch, like a shaped explosive. These questions have to be clear, concise, sharp, and cutting in order to separate the innocent from the guilty, the deceivers from the truth-tellers. The cutline between the two often requires the precision of a diamond cutter. The more time spent on the structure of critical questions, the better.

Simpson: We were leaving a dance recital. She took off and I was talking to her parents.

There was no discussion about what happened the night before (the night of the killings) up to this point. This is the beginning of Lange and Vannatter's attempt to reconstruct where O.J. was the night before. This is a very critical question.

O.J. responds to this very specific time request with, "We were leaving," which is not time specific. A response of, "We left," would be much more responsive. Also note that Vannatter asked for "the last time," not, "the last place." Instead of a time, O.J. responds with, "a dance recital," which isn't a time. It's not even an approximation of a time. A response like "the dance recital," or "we left a dance recital last night," would have been much more responsive, but still not sufficient. With the response, "We were leaving a dance recital," O.J. is being non-specific, general, and imprecise. His answer is not definitive or finite. It's not a clear, simple, or precise response.

Remember, O.J. is being questioned about murdering two people. He knows he's a suspect in those murders. This question is critical in determining when he "last saw" Nicole. If you were asked this question and you didn't commit the homicides, you would make sure you provided a specific, precise answer, saying, "7:30 PM," or "When we left the dance recital last night." You would want to prove your innocence. You wouldn't be imprecise and careless and say, "We were leaving a dance recital." He (O.J.'s Alvin) substitutes an "a" for "the" and it provides O.J. with ambiguity and intentional obfuscation to avoid telling a complete lie (Chapter 2). If he were the killer, he would be telling a complete lie to answer, "When we left the dance recital." A truth teller would use "the" not an "a." Deception is designed to be subtle, almost imperceptible. This is deception.

Also, the "took" in "She took off" suggests a lot of emotion. He could have said, "She went" or "She left" but O.J. chose "took." This suggests anger and/or emotion before she departed. The words "left" or "went" reflect much less emotion. Also, "talking to her parents" is not a direct response to the question, it is a deflection. Pay particular attention to deflections. They are evidence of sensitivity to the question and an attempt to fill the time and take the interview off track. I like the question and the timing of it. I would like a better-worded critical question. And they needed to force O.J. to respond with clarity and precision to get the truth.

Vannatter: Where was the dance recital?

Simpson: Paul Revere High School.

Vannatter: And was that for one of your children?

Simpson: Yeah, for my daughter Sydney.

Vannatter: And what time was that yesterday?

Simpson: It ended about 6:30, quarter to seven, something like that, you know, in the ballpark, right in that area. And they took off.

This is a larger than necessary explanation on the time. A simple, "About 6:30," would have sufficed but instead we get this lengthy, vague response. This is cause for suspicion. And, he says, ". . . they took off." Earlier he said, "She took off." Who is the "they" and why is there now someone else with Nicole?

Vannatter: They?

Vannatter picks up on the new pronoun. It's interesting now that he includes the parents "took off" description.

Simpson: Her and her family — her mother and father, sisters, my kids, you know.

Vannatter: And then you went your own separate way?

Simpson: Yeah, actually she left, and then they came back and her mother got in a car with her, and the kids all piled into her sister's car, and they . . .

So, now he provides more details. "She left," not took off, "and then they came back." A good question now would be who is "they." It appears as though Nicole "took off" or "left" and then "they" came back. This needs explanation.

Vannatter: Was Nicole driving?

Simpson: Yeah.

Vannatter: What kind of car was she driving?

Simpson: Her black car, a Cherokee, a Jeep Cherokee.

Vannatter: What were you driving?

Simpson: My Rolls-Royce, my Bentley.

Vannatter: Do you own that Ford Bronco that sits outside?

Simpson: Hertz owns it, and Hertz lets me use it.

Vannatter: So that's your vehicle, the one that was parked there on the street?

Simpson: Mmm hmm.

***Again, not a "yes." Remember, the Bronco is critical because that is the source of all the forensic evidence used in the trial. Note that O.J. is admitting that the Bronco is "the one that was parked there on the street." Only O.J. would know if the Bronco was parked on the street! This is extremely important because it shows that O.J. knew it was parked where it was found on the street and he was the last one to have parked it there!

Vannatter: And it's actually owned by Hertz?

Simpson: Hertz, yeah.

Vannatter: Who's the primary driver on that? You?

Simpson: I drive it, the housekeeper drives it, you know, it's kind of a . . .

Vannatter: All-purpose type vehicle?

Simpson: All-purpose, yeah. It's the only one that my insurance will allow me to let anyone else drive.

Vannatter: OK.

Lange: When you drive it, where do you park it at home? Where it is now, it was in the street or something?

Unnecessary and ill-advised compound question. Questions need to be simple, direct, and well defined.

Simpson: I always park it on the street.

Lange: You never take it in the . . .

Simpson: Oh, rarely. I mean, I'll bring it in — and switch the stuff, you know, and stuff like that. I did that yesterday, you know.

Lange: When did you last drive it?

Simpson: Yesterday.

Vannatter: What time yesterday?

Simpson: In the morning, in the afternoon.

Which is it? The morning or the afternoon, or both? As a questioner, you can't leave an answer like this. If you do,you tell the subject that ambiguous answers are acceptable and tolerated. The subject will take advantage of this. It's kind of a training process, wherein the questioner sets the tone for all to follow. If the questioner allows imprecision, the subject will take advantage of that. Now, this may be a strategy by the questioner, in which case it needs to be a good one. One that needs to have good follow up.

Vannatter: OK, you left her, you're saying, about 6:30 or 7, or she left the recital?

Simpson: Yeah.

Vannatter: And you spoke with her parents?

Simpson: Yeah, we were just sitting there talking.

Vannatter: OK, what time did you leave the recital?

Simpson: Right about that time. We were all leaving. We were all leaving then. Her mother said something about me joining them for dinner, and I said no thanks.

Vannatter: Where did you go from there, O.J.?

Good question.

Simpson: Ah, home, home for a while, got my car for a while, tried to find my girlfriend for a while, came back to the house.

Take careful note of this verbiage. "Ah, home, home for a while, got my car for a while, tried to find my girlfriend for a while, came back to the house." Not one single pronoun in there! No pronoun, especially no "I" means no commitment. We will return to this later when he is again asked about this and he inserts the pronoun "I" but with an introduction — which makes the "I" meaningless. This statement is the only one we can rely on.

Again, the questioner needs to demand precision. As you'll see later, O.J. (Alvin) uses this answer very, very artfully in a later deceptive answer on page 124, see where he states,

Simpson: "Over at about 6:30. <u>Like I said, I came home, I got my car, I was going to see my girlfriend.</u> I was calling her and she wasn't around."

Why did O.J. add personal pronouns to this later statement for this critical time period? Because he can now add credulity to the statement by adding his "I" now when he couldn't earlier. He did say, "home, home for a while, got my car for a while, tried to fiend my girlfriend for a while, . . ." Since he said that earlier, he can now use an "I" with the all important introduction, "Like I said. . . ." This is "deception by referral," and is an important indicator of deception. If we were to view this statement alone, out of context, we may think he was being truthful. Context is very important. Introductions are extremely important.

Vannatter: Who was home when you got home?

Simpson: Kato.

How does he know that? Follow up questions needed here.

Vannatter: Kato? Anybody else? Was your daughter there, Arnelle?

Simpson: No.

Vannatter: Isn't that her name, Arnelle?

Simpson: Arnelle, yeah.

Vannatter: So what time do you think you got back home, actually physically got home?

GETTING THE TRUTH

Never use the word "think" in a question, it allows ambiguity and unnecessary "wiggle" responses.

Simpson: Seven-something.

Vague.

Vannatter: Seven-something? And then you left, and . . .

Simpson: Yeah, I'm trying to think, did I leave? You know, I'm always . . . I had to run and get my daughter some flowers. I was actually doing the recital, so I rushed and got her some flowers, and I came home, and then I called Paula as I was going to her house, and Paula wasn't home.

When the subject repeats a question, it is <u>always</u> worth a closer look.

Vannatter: Paula is your girlfriend?

Simpson: Girlfriend, yeah.

Vannatter: Paula who?

Simpson: Barbieri.

Vannatter: Could you spell that for me?

Simpson: B-A-R-B-I-E-R-I.

Vannatter: Do you know an address on her?

Simpson: No, she lives on Wilshire, but I think she's out of town.

Vannatter: You got a phone number?

Simpson: Yeah (number deleted by STAR).

Vannatter: So you didn't see her last night?

Simpson: No, we'd been to a big affair the night before, and then I came back home. I was basically at home. I mean, any time I was . . . whatever time it took me to get to the recital and back, to get to the flower shop and back, I mean, that's the time I was out of the house.

The word "see" in the question bothers me. What does "see" mean? We already know O.J. is being deceptive, so be careful not to help him. A better way of phrasing this question would be, "So, were you together last night with Paula?"

"I was basically at home," is, by now, a typically vague and unresponsive answer. These kinds of answers have been allowed before in this interview and they will continue, because they are allowed. As a questioner, you need to set the tone early to "train" or "force" the subject to answer with precision. Precise questioning is the antidote to deceptive responses. You need to nail the subject down with precise questioning. Remember, he's being asked for details as to where he was when the homicides took place and he responds with, "... basically at home?" Then he follows that up with nervous, vague, and superfluous comments.

Vannatter: Were you scheduled to play golf this morning, some place?

Simpson: In Chicago.

Vannatter: What kind of tournament was it?

Simpson: Ah, it was Hertz, with special clients.

Vannatter: Oh, OK. What time did you leave last night, leave the house?

Simpson: To go to the airport?

Why must this be clarified?

Vannatter: Mmm hmm.

Simpson: About . . . the limo was supposed to be there at 10:45. Normally, they get there a little earlier. I was rushing around — somewhere between there and 11.

This should have been a simple, clear answer. Instead, we get a vague and difficult response. Why was he rushing around?

Vannatter: So approximately 10:45 to 11.

Simpson: Eleven o'clock, yea, somewhere in that area.

Vannatter: And you went by limo?

Simpson: Yeah.

Vannatter: Who's the limo service?

Simpson: Ah, you have to ask my office.

Lange: Did you converse with the driver at all? Did you talk to him?

Simpson: No, he was a new driver. Normally, I have a regular driver I drive with and converse. No, just about rushing to the airport, about how I live my life on airplanes, and hotels, that type of thing.

Lange: What time did the plane leave?

Simpson: Ah, 11:45 the flight took off.

Vannatter: What airline was it?

Simpson: American.

Vannatter: American? And it was 11:45 to Chicago?

Simpson: Chicago.

Lange: So yesterday you did drive the white Bronco?

Simpson: Mmm hmm.

Lange now and a non "yes" answer.

Lange: And where did you park it when you brought it home?

Simpson: Ah, the first time probably by the mailbox. I'm trying to think, or did I bring it in the driveway? Normally, I will park it by the mailbox, sometimes . . .

Lange: On Ashford, or Ashland?

Simpson: On Ashford, yeah.

Lange: Where did you park yesterday for the last time, do you remember?

Questions should never include, "do you remember?" That allows wiggle room and the word "remember" should never be included in questions, ever.

Simpson: Right where it is.

***And here is the confirmation that O.J. and O.J. alone was the last to drive the Bronco and where the Bronco was found was where he and he alone parked it. Nothing else explains his confidence that the Bronco was found where he parked it — "Right where it is." This is an admission that was never introduced and never explored further.

Lange: Where it is now?

Simpson: Yeah.

Lange: Where, on . . .?

Simpson: Right on the street there.

Lange: On Ashford?

Simpson: No, on Rockingham.

Lange: You parked it there?

Simpson: Yes.

Lange: About what time was that?

Simpson: Eight-something, seven . . . eight, nine o'clock, I don't know, right in that area.

Now he is waffling on the time he got home. Earlier he said "seven something." Now, it's "eight-something, seven, eight, nine o'clock, I don't know." There are many, many clues that he doesn't want to get pinned down on the time he parked that Bronco for the last time and returned home.

Lange: Did you take it to the recital?

Simpson: No.

He already stated he drove the Bentley to the recital.

Lange: What time was the recital?

Simpson: Over at about 6:30. Like I said, I came home, I got my car, I was going to see my girlfriend. I was calling her and she wasn't around.

Here's the section I referred to earlier. Notice now he is able to insert the pronoun "I" that Alvin couldn't use earlier. The reason he can commit to this now is because of his introduction: "Like I said, . . ." He did say that before. So, Alvin justifies the "I" now because he did say it before. This is called Deception by Referral. The introduction is the key and if you don't hear it or notice it, you could easily misinterpret this response. The key is to go back to the original statement (in this case on page 118). We need to rely on the original statement. In this case, there is no "I" in the original statement therefore we cannot rely on it. The fact he now inserts an "I" is further evidence of deception.

Lange: So you drove the . . . you came home in the Rolls, and then you got in the Bronco . . .

Simpson: In the Bronco, 'cause my phone was in the Bronco. And because it's a Bronco. It's a Bronco, it's what I drive, you know. I'd rather drive it than any other car. And, you know, as I was going over there, I called her a couple of times and she wasn't there, and I left a message, and then I checked my messages, and there were no new messages. She wasn't there, and she may have to leave town. Then I came back and ended up sitting with Kato.

Lange: OK, what time was this again that you parked the Bronco?

Simpson: Eight-something, maybe. He hadn't done a Jacuzzi, we had . . . went and got a burger, and I'd come home and kind of leisurely got ready to go. I mean, we'd done a few things . . .

Lange: You weren't in a hurry when you came back with the Bronco.

Simpson: No.

Lange: The reason I asked you, the cars were parked kind of at a funny angle, stuck out in the street.

Simpson: Well, it's parked because . . . I don't know if it's a funny angle or what. It's parked because when I was hustling at the end of the day to get all my stuff, and I was getting my phone and everything off it, when I just pulled it out of the gate there, it's like it's a tight turn.

Always look closely at incomplete responses or thought processes, *"Well, it's parked because . . . I don't know . . .* These can be windows into what the subject is really thinking. They're flags that show where Alvin is having difficulty constructing an answer.

Lange: So you had it inside the compound, then?

Simpson: Yeah.

Lange: Oh, OK.

Simpson: I brought it inside the compound to get my stuff out of it, and then I put it out, and I'd run back inside the gate before the gate closes.

Look closely at the change in tenses here. I always look for first person singular, past tense when people describe past events. Anything else is suspicious. He gives a first person singular, past tense "I brought it inside the compound to get my stuff out of it, and then I put it out." But then he changes tenses by saying, "I'd run back inside the gate before the gate closes." A change in tenses is very, very important. In this case, he's describing what happened, then changes to what would normally happen. This is an indication of deception. Then you ask yourself, why? Why would this subject be deceptive when being asked a simple question about the Bronco and what he did with it?

Vannatter: What's you office phone number?

Simpson: (number deleted by STAR)

Vannatter: And is that area code 310?

Simpson: Yes.

Again, note he's able to answer with a simple "Yes," and nothing more.

Vannatter: How did you get the injury on your hand?

Simpson: I don't know. The first time, when I was in Chicago and all, but at the house I was just running around.

This is a vague and suspicious answer. The "I don't know" could have been sufficient but may be deemed suspicious, so he adds the almost incomprehensible explanation.

Vannatter: How did you do it in Chicago?

Simpson: I broke a glass. One of you guys had just called me, and I was in the bathroom, and I just kind of went bonkers for a little bit.

Lange: Is that how you cut it?

Simpson: Mmm, it was cut before, but I think I just opened it again, I'm not sure.

GETTING THE TRUTH

He states that his hand was cut before. Then, he states, "... but I think I just opened it again, I'm not sure." This doesn't make sense and he knows it.

Lange: Do you recall bleeding at all in your truck, in the Bronco?

Never use "recall" in your questions.

Simpson: I recall bleeding at my house and then I went to the Bronco. The last thing I did before I left, when I was rushing, was went and got my phone out of the Bronco.

Lange: Mmm hmm. Where's the phone now?

Simpson: In my bag.

Lange: You have it . . .?

Simpson: In that black bag.

Lange: You brought a bag with you here?

Simpson: Yeah, it's . . .

Lange: So do you recall bleeding at all?

Simpson: Yeah, I mean, I knew I was bleeding, but it was no big deal. I bleed all the time. I play golf and stuff, so there's always something, nicks and stuff here and there.

Lange: So did you do anything? When did you put the Band-Aid on it?

Simpson: Actually, I asked the girl this morning for it.

Lange: And she got it?

Simpson: Yeah, 'cause last night with Kato, when I was leaving, he was saying something to me, and I was rushing to get my phone, and I put a little thing on it, and it stopped.

Vannatter: Do you have the keys to that Bronco?

Simpson: Yeah.

Again, not a "yes," answer, so notable.

Vannatter: OK. We've impounded the Bronco. I don't know if you know that or not.

Simpson: No.

Vannatter: . . . take a look at it. Other than you, who's the last person to drive it.

Simpson: Probably Gigi. When I'm out of town, I don't know who drives the car, maybe my daughter, maybe Kato.

Vannatter: The keys are available?

Simpson: I leave the keys there, you know, when Gigi's there because sometimes she needs it, or Gigi was off and wasn't coming back until today, and I was coming back tonight.

Vannatter: So you don't mind if Gigi uses it, or . . .

Simpson: This is the only one I can let her use. When she doesn't have her car, 'cause sometimes her husband takes her car, I let her use the car.

Lange: When was the last time you were at Nicole's house?

Simpson: I don't go in, I won't go in her house. I haven't been in her house in a week, maybe five days. I go to her house a lot. I mean, I'm always dropping the kids off, picking the kids up, fooling around with the dog, you know.

The question was, "When is the last time you were at Nicole's house?" His answer is not responsive, and therefore suspicious.

Vannatter: How does that usually work? Do you drop them at the porch, or do you go in with them?

Simpson: No, I don't go in the house.

Vannatter: Is there a kind of gate out front?

Simpson: Yeah.

Vannatter: But you never go inside the house?

Simpson: Up until about five days, six days ago, I haven't been in the house. Once I started seeing Paula again, I kind of avoid Nicole.

This is intentionally obfuscated. Interesting that he would infer that he had been inside the house after "five days, six days ago . . ." What would have caused that, given that he emphatically stated earlier that he doesn't go into her house. This should be explored through further questioning.

Vannatter: Is Nicole seeing anybody else that you . . .

Simpson: I have no idea. I really have absolutely no idea. I don't ask her. I don't know. Her and her girlfriends, they go out, you know, they've got some things going on right now with her girlfriends, so I'm assuming something's happening because one of the girlfriends is having a big problem with her husband because she's always saying she's with Nicole until three or four in the morning. She's not. You know, Nicole tells me she leaves her at 1:30 or 2 or 2:30, and the girl doesn't get home until 5, and she only lives a few blocks away.

He provides an unusually long, involved explanation to a question that could have been answered with a simple, "I don't know." This is one of the longest response (if not the longest) in the whole interview. Why? He states, emphatically, "She's not" when addressing whether Nicole is out with one of her girlfriends until 3 or 4 in the morning. How can he be so sure? The emphatic way it's stated reveals personal knowledge, not hearsay. He tries to obscure this emphatic statement by inferring that he knows because Nicole told him. That personal knowledge needs to be explored. The first thing I'd look at is whether there is any evidence he surveilled Nicole to see when she arrived home after nights out with her girlfriends.

Vannatter: Something's going on, huh?

Lange: Do you know where they went, the family, for dinner last night?

Simpson: No. Well, no, I didn't ask.

Another curious answer. Why not leave it at "No." He can't because Alvin won't allow it. He qualifies it with, "Well, no, I didn't ask." That qualifier clarifies the "No," to mean no one told him — but now leaves open whether he had personal knowledge. Look closely and try to follow this analysis. A simple "No" would include any and all options. A

"No" followed by the qualifier allows him to answer with a "No" and not include personal knowledge. Another deceptive answer which is constructed to mislead the questioner to believe he's answered "No" to the question, when, in fact, he has not.

Lange: I just thought maybe there's a regular place that they go.

Simpson: No. If I was with them, we'd go to Toscano. I mean, not Toscano, Poponi's.

Vannatter: You haven't had any problems with her lately, have you, O.J.?

Simpson: I always have problems with her, you know? Our relationship has been a problem relationship. Probably lately for me, and I say this only because I said it to Ron yesterday at the — Ron Fishman, whose wife is Cora — at the dance recital, when he came up to me and went, "Oooh, boy, what's going on?" and everybody was beefing with everybody. And I said, "Well, I'm just glad I'm out of the mix." You know, because I was like dealing with him and his problems with his wife and Nicole and evidently some new problems that a guy named Christian was having with his girl, and he was staying at Nicole's house, and something was going on, but I don't think it's pertinent to this.

Another lengthy, emotional, vague, and unresponsive answer. We would expect emotion to be a big part of this entire interview. After all, his wife of several years has just been killed. Now, he reveals he knows a "guy named Christian" was staying at Nicole's house. How did he know that?

Vannatter: Did Nicole have words with you last night?

Simpson: Pardon me?

A question answered by a question is always suspicious, unless you can attribute that to a clarification or hearing issue.

Vannatter: Did Nicole have words with you last night?

Simpson: No, not at all.

Remember, the Nicole "took off" discussion.

Vannatter: Did you talk to her last night?

Simpson: To ask to speak to my daughter, to congratulate my daughter, and everything.

Vannatter: But you didn't have a conversation with her?

Simpson: No, no.

Not a simple "no." Ask yourself, why? A singular "no" would be sufficient. Since a simple "no" is sufficient, a double "no" is suspicious.

Vannatter: What were you wearing last night, O.J.?

Simpson: What did I wear on the golf course yesterday? Some of these kind of pants, some of these kind of pants — I mean I changed different for whatever it was. I just had on some . . .

GETTING THE TRUTH

This is not a difficult question, but the answer is a question, and then a vague, unreasonably vague response.

Vannatter: Just these black pants.

Simpson: Just these . . . They're called Bugle Boy.

Vannatter: These aren't the pants?

Simpson: No.

Vannatter: Where are the pants that you wore?

Simpson: They're hanging in my closet.

This is a simple direct response.

Vannatter: These are washable, right? You just throw them in the laundry?

Simpson: Yeah, I got 100 pair. They give them to me free, Bugle Boys, so I've got a bunch of them.

Vannatter: Do you recall coming home and hanging them up, or...?

Simpson: I always hang up my clothes. I mean, it's rare that I don't hang up my clothes unless I'm laying them in my bathroom for her to do something with them, but those are the only things I don't hang up. But when you play golf, you don't necessarily dirty pants.

This is a well crafted, complex response. Alvin is proud of this one. Simple, direct responses are desirable and more truthful. He's already stated, "Yeah," to Vannatter's, "You just throw them in the laundry?" But it was a two-part question, so we're not sure what his answer means. Earlier, he stated about his pants that he wore the night before, "They're hanging in my closet." Further, his statement "I always" does not equate to "I hung them up." It equates to what he "always" does not to what he did. Therefore, without further questioning O.J. has successfully muddled and so obfuscated his responses that we can't draw defendable conclusions.

Lange: What kind of shoes were you wearing?

Simpson: Tennis shoes.

Lange: Tennis shoes? Do you know what kind?

Simpson: Probably Reebok, that's all I wear.

"Probably" is not a direct, simple response. It is intentionally vague.

Lange: Are they at home, too?

Simpson: Yeah

Not a "yes."

Lange: Was this supposed to be a short trip to Chicago, so you didn't take a whole lot?

Questions should never offer an answer. Simply ask the question and wait for the response. There are several examples in this exercise where the question itself contaminated the response. Look at the question, then look to see if O.J. uses the exact word in his response. And, there are cases where he is unaware of what the word means and O.J.'s answer doesn't show an understanding of the word "arrested" like Lange intended (see page 110, where Lange asks: " *Lange:* Were you arrested at one time for something?"). That is contamination, and to avoid it, you need to make sure the subject understands the word in the same way the questioner understands it. That's sometimes difficult to do, so you need to look for signs of understanding in earlier or subsequent responses.

Simpson: Yeah, I was coming back today.

Lange: Just overnight?

Simpson: Yeah.

Vannatter: That's a hectic schedule, drive back here to play golf and come back.

Simpson: Yeah, but I do it all the time.

Vannatter: Do you?

Simpson: Yeah. That's what I was complaining with the driver about, you know, about my whole life is on and off airplanes.

Vannatter: O.J., we've got sort of a problem.

Simpson: Mmm hmm.

Curious response.

Vannatter: We've got some blood on and in your car, we've got some blood at your house, and sort of a problem.

Simpson: Well, take my blood test.

Another curious response.

Lange: Well, we'd like to do that. We've got, of course, the cut on your finger that you aren't real clear on. Do you recall having that cut on

your finger the last time you were at Nicole's
house?

Simpson: A week ago?

This is an even more curious response. A person who had
been at Nicole's house a week ago the last time wouldn't ask
this question. There would be no reason to ask that question,
because in his mind there would be no other options as to
when he had last been there. Perhaps, I suppose, he could
later argue that Lange was referring to when he was there two
weeks ago or three weeks ago. But let's remember why O.J. is
being interviewed. He's being interviewed about the homicide
that occurred the night before. He knows he's a suspect, the
officers gave him a Miranda warning. So, it's very unlikely O.J.
would be thinking about something other than the night of the
homicide. So, his response, "A week ago?" is very suspicious.

Lange: Yeah.

Simpson: No. It was last night.

A simple, direct and emphatic response, "No. It was last
night?" Why earlier did he say, "A week ago?" Now, he is sure,
emphatically sure. Why?

Lange: OK, so last night you cut it.

Vannatter: Somewhere after the recital?

Simpson: Somewhere when I was rushing to get out
of my house.

Vannatter: OK, after the recital.

Simpson: Yeah.

Vannatter: What do you think happened? Do you have any idea?

Simpson: I have no idea, man. You guys haven't told me anything. I have no idea. When you said to my daughter, who said something to me today, that somebody else might have been involved, I have absolutely no idea what happened. I don't know how, why or what. But you guys haven't told me anything. Every time I ask you guys, you say you're going to tell me in a bit.

Vannatter: Well, we don't know a lot of answers to these questions yet ourselves, O.J., OK?

Simpson: I've got a bunch of guns, guns all over the place. You can take them, they're all there. I mean, you can see them. I keep them in my car for an incident that happened a month ago that my in-laws, my wife and everybody knows about that.

Vannatter: What was that?

Simpson: Going down to . . . and cops down there know about it because I've told two marshals about it. At a mall, I was going down for a christening, and I had just left — and it was like 3:30 in the morning, and I'm in a lane, and also the car in front of me is going real slow, and I'm slowing down 'cause I figure he sees a cop, 'cause we were all going pretty fast. And I'm going to change lanes, but there's a car next to me, and I can't change lanes. Then that goes for a while, and I'm going to slow down and go around him but the car butts up to me, and I'm like caught between three cars. They were Oriental guys, and they were not letting me go anywhere. And finally I went on the shoulder, and I sped up, and then I held my phone up so they could see the light part of it, you know, 'cause I have tinted windows, and they kind of scattered, and I chased one of them for a while to make him think I was chasing him before I took off.

Lange: Were you in the Bronco?

Simpson: No.

Lange: What were you driving?

Simpson: My Bentley. It has tinted windows and all, so I figured they thought they had a nice little touch...

Lange: Did you think they were trying to rip you off?

Simpson: Definitely, they were. And then the next thing, you know, Nicole and I went home. At four in the morning I got there to Laguna, and when we woke up, I told her about it, and told her parents about it, told everybody about it, you know? And when I saw two marshals at a mall, I walked up and told them about it.

Vannatter: What did they do, make a report on it?

Simpson: They didn't know nothing. I mean, they'll remember me and remember I told them.

Vannatter: Did Nicole mention that she'd been getting any threats lately to you? Anything she was concerned about or the kids' safety?

Simpson: To her?

A reasonable question this time.

Vannatter: Yes.

Simpson: From?

This is not a reasonable response. The question he is being asked is whether Nicole mentioned if she had been getting threats and he replies, "From?" If this question is asked of an ex-husband who was not involved in the homicide, this should be an easy "yes" or "no." Instead, O.J. responds with a question.

Vannatter: From anybody.

Simpson: No, not at all.

Again, a simple no is best.

Vannatter: Was she very security conscious? Did she keep that house locked up?

Simpson: Very.

Vannatter: The intercom didn't work apparently, right?

Simpson: I thought it worked.

Vannatter: Oh, OK. Does the electronic buzzer work?

Simpson: The electronic buzzer works to let people in.

Vannatter: Do you ever park in the rear when you go over there?

Simpson: Most of the time.

Vannatter: You do park in the rear.

Simpson: Most times when I'm taking the kids there, I come right into the driveway, blow the horn, and she, or a lot of times the housekeeper, either the housekeeper opens or they'll keep a garage door open up on the top of the thing, you know, but that's when I'm dropping the kids off, and I'm not going in. — times I go to the front because the kids have to hit the buzzer and stuff.

Vannatter: Did you say before that up until about three weeks ago you guys were going out again and trying to . . .

Simpson: No, we'd been going out for about a year, and then the last six months we've had . . . it ain't been working, so we tried various things to see if we can make it work. We started trying to date, and that wasn't working, and so, you know, we just said the hell with it, you know.

Vannatter: And that was about three weeks ago?

Simpson: Yeah, about three weeks ago.

Vannatter: So you were seeing her up to that point?

Simpson: It's, it's . . . seeing her, yeah, I mean, yeah. It was a done deal. It just wasn't happening. I mean, I was gone. I was in San Juan doing a film, and I don't think we had sex since I've been back from San Juan, and that was like two months ago. So it's been like . . . for the kids we tried to do things together, you know, we didn't really date each other. Then we decided let's try to date each other. We went out one night, and it just didn't work.

An emotional response, and an enlightening one.

Vannatter: When you say it didn't work, what do you mean?

Simpson: Ah, the night we went out it was fun. Then the next night we went out it was actually when I was down in Laguna, and she didn't want to go out. And I said, "Well, let's go out 'cause I came all the way down here to go out," and we kind of had a beef. And it just didn't work after that, you know? We were only trying to date to see if we could bring some romance back into our relationship. We just said, let's treat each other like boyfriend and girlfriend instead of, you know, like 17-year-old married people. I mean, 17 years together, whatever that is.

Vannatter: How long were you together?

Simpson: Seventeen years.

Vannatter: Seventeen years. Did you ever hit her, O.J.?

Simpson: Ah, one night we had a fight. We had a fight, and she hit me. And they never took my statement, they never wanted to hear my side, and they never wanted to hear the housekeeper's side. Nicole was drunk. She did her thing, she started tearing up my house, you know? I didn't punch her or anything, but I . . .

The simple "No" is missing.

Vannatter: . . . slapped her a couple of times.

Simpson: No, no, I wrestled her, is what I did. I didn't slap her at all. I mean, Nicole's a strong girl. She's a . . . one of the most conditioned women. Since that period of time, she's hit me a few times, but I've never touched her after that, and I'm telling you, it's five-six years ago.

Note the, ". . . and I'm telling you, it's five-six years ago." An introduction that should tell you not to rely on what follows.

The simple "No" is missing.

Now, I'll leave the remainder of this statement to you without my commentary. By now you have established a foundation for how the subject responds to questions and how he doesn't. You also have my analysis. You have the basis for getting the truth from his answers. Give it a try and see how you do.

Vannatter: What is her birth date?

Simpson: May 19th.

Vannatter: Did you get together with her on her birthday?

Simpson: Yeah, her and I and the kids, I believe.

Vannatter: Did you give her a gift?

Simpson: I gave her a gift.

Vannatter: What did you give her?

GETTING THE TRUTH

Simpson: I gave her either a bracelet or the earrings.

Vannatter: Did she keep them or . . .

Simpson: Oh, no, when we split she gave me both the earrings and the bracelet back. I bought her a very nice bracelet — I don't know if it was Mother's Day or her birthday — and I bought her the earrings for the other thing, and when we split — and it's a credit to her — she felt that it wasn't right that she had it, and I said good because I want them back.

Vannatter: Was that the very day of her birthday, May 19, or was it a few days later?

Simpson: What do you mean?

Vannatter: You gave it to her on the 19th of May, her birthday, right, this bracelet?

Simpson: I may have given her the earrings. No, the bracelet, May 19th. When was Mother's Day?

Vannatter: Mother's Day was around that . . .

Simpson: No, it was probably her birthday, yes.

Vannatter: And did she return it the same day?

Simpson: Oh, no, she . . . I'm in a funny place here on this, all right? She returned it — both of them — three weeks ago or so, because when I say I'm in a funny place on this it was because I gave it to my girlfriend and told her it was for her, and that was three weeks ago. I told her I bought it for her. You know? What am I going to do with it?

Lange: Did Mr. Weitzman, your attorney, talk to you anything about this polygraph we brought up before? What are your thoughts on that?

Simpson: Should I talk about my thoughts on that? I'm sure eventually I'll do it, but it's like I've got some weird thoughts now. I've had weird thoughts . . . you know when you've been with a person for 17 years, you think everything. I've got to understand what this thing is. If it's true blue, I don't mind doing it.

Lange: Well, you're not compelled at all to take this thing, number one, and number two — I don't know if Mr. Weitzman explained it to you — this goes to the exclusion of someone as much as the inclusion so we can eliminate people. And just to get things straight.

Simpson: But does it work for elimination?

Lange: Oh, yes. We use it for elimination more than anything.

Simpson: Well, I'll talk to him about it.

Lange: Understand, the reason we're talking to you is because you're the ex-husband.

Simpson: I know, I'm the number one target, and now you tell me I've got blood all over the place.

Lange: Well, there's blood at your house in the driveway, and we've got a search warrant, and we're going to go get the blood. We found some in your house. Is that your blood that's there?

GETTING THE TRUTH

Simpson: If it's dripped, it's what I dripped running around trying to leave.

Lange: Last night?

Simpson: Yeah, and I wasn't aware that it was . . . I was aware that I . . . You know, I was trying to get out of the house. I didn't even pay any attention to it, I saw it when I was in the kitchen, and I grabbed a napkin or something, and that was it. I didn't think about it after that.

Vannatter: That was last night after you got home from the recital, when you were rushing?

Simpson: That was last night when I was . . . I don't know what I was . . . I was in the car getting my junk out of the car. I was in the house throwing hangers and stuff in my suitcase. I was doing my little crazy what I do . . . I mean, I do it everywhere. Anybody who has ever picked me up says that O.J.'s a whirlwind, he's running, he's grabbing things, and that's what I was doing.

Vannatter: Well, I'm going to step out and I'm going to get a photographer to come down and photograph your hand there. And then here pretty soon we're going to take you downstairs and get some blood from you. OK? I'll be right back.

Lange: So it was about five days ago you last saw Nicole? Was it at the house?

Simpson: OK, the last time I saw Nicole, physically saw Nicole . . . I saw her obviously last night.

The time before, I'm trying to think . . . I went to Washington, DC, so I didn't see her, so I'm trying to think . . . I haven't seen her since I went to Washington — what's the date today?

Lange: Today's Monday, the 13th of June.

Simpson: OK, I went to Washington on maybe Wednesday. Thursday I think I was in . . . Thursday I was in Connecticut, then Long Island Thursday afternoon and all of Friday. I got home Friday night, Friday afternoon. I played, you know . . . Paula picked me up at the airport. I played golf Saturday, and when I came home I think my son was there. So I did something with my son. I don't think I saw Nicole at all then. And then I went to a big affair with Paula Saturday night, and I got up and played golf Sunday which pissed Paula off, and I saw Nicole at . . . It was about a week before, I saw her at the . . .

Lange: OK, the last time you saw Nicole, was that at her house?

Simpson: I don't remember. I wasn't in her house, so it couldn't have been at her house, so it was, you know, I don't physically remember the last time I saw her. I may have seen her even jogging one day.

Lange: Let me get this straight. You've never physically been inside the house?

Simpson: Not in the last week.

Lange: Ever. I mean, how long has she lived there? About six months?

Simpson: Oh, Christ, I've slept at the house many, many, many times, you know? I've done everything at the house, you know? I'm just saying, . . . You're talking in the last week or so.

Lange: Well, whatever. Six months she's lived there?

Simpson: I don't know. Roughly. I was at her house maybe two weeks ago, 10 days ago. One night her and I had a long talk, you know, about how can we make it better for the kids, and I told her we'd do things better. And, OK, I can almost say when that was. That was when I . . . I don't know, it was about 10 days ago. And then we . . . The next day I had her have her dog do a flea bath or something with me. Oh, I'll tell you, I did see her one day. One day I went . . . I don't know if this was the early part of last week, I went 'cause my son had to go and get something, and he ran in, and she came to the gate, and the dog ran out, and her friend Faye and I went looking for the dog. That may have been a week ago, I don't know.

Lange: (To Vannatter) Got a photographer coming?

Vannatter: No, we're going to take him up there.

Lange: We're ready to terminate this at 14:07.

13B
AN OPEN LETTER TO WASHINGTON
12/9/2013

I've included my analysis of this letter for several reasons. One, it will help you see the true agenda in letters written to you or your business in the future. Secondly, it may help you when you are constructing letters to make sure you don't make the same mistakes. Thirdly, I just enjoy dismantling poorly written letters by billionaires who have the money to hire the best writers in the world.

Dear Mr. President and Members of Congress,

We understand that governments have a duty to protect their citizens. But this summer's revelations highlighted the urgent need to reform government surveillance practices worldwide. The balance in many countries has tipped too far in favor of the state and away from the rights of the individual — rights that are enshrined in our Constitution. This undermines the freedoms we all cherish. It's time for a change.

For our part, we are focused on keeping users' data secure — deploying the latest encryption technology to prevent unauthorized surveillance on our networks and by pushing back on government requests to ensure that they are legal and reasonable in scope.

We urge the US to take the lead and make reforms that ensure that government surveillance efforts are clearly restricted by law, proportionate to the risks, transparent and subject to independent oversight. To see the full set of principles we support, visit ReformGovernmentSurveillance.com

Sincerely,

AOL, Apple, Facebook, Google, LinkedIn, Microsoft, Twitter, Yahoo

ANALYSIS:

Dear Mr. President and Members of Congress, *(very specific, excludes Supreme Court)*

We (who? These clearly are entities and these views don't necessarily represent the views of all employees, shareholders, etc.) *understand (this is loaded with misunderstanding) that governments have a duty to protect their citizens.* (A very simple statement that requires a great deal more explanation. While directing this message to the U.S. Government, by stating "governments" they include all governments, not just the U.S. Government. This creates confusion as to whom this is directed). *But* (always inflammatory) *this summer's revelations* (unspecified) *highlighted the* (not "an," or "a," but "the") *urgent need to reform government surveillance practices worldwide* (Since there is no "our government" or "U.S. Government," is this directed to all governments?). *The* (again, a shift to worldwide) *balance* (again, a loaded word that requires much more explanation) *in many countries* (again, a worldwide directive) *has tipped too far* (judgmental without stating evidence to support) *in favor of the state* (judgmental, and again all governments) *and away from the rights of the individual — rights that are enshrined in our Constitution* (mixing our Constitutional rights with International rights). *This undermines the freedoms we all cherish.* (a statement without an established base). *It's time for a* (connotes specificity as opposed to a solution. This reveals the desire for a specific solution, showing the writers have their own agenda. They aren't looking for a "solution" [which involves rigorous review; rather they are looking for a *"change,"* which doesn't require rigor] *change.*

For our part (why this?), *we are focused on keeping users' data secure — deploying the latest encryption technology to prevent unauthorized surveillance* on (interesting that this is "on" and not "of," which would include internal surveillance as opposed to "on" which connotes external surveillance) *our networks and by pushing back on government requests to ensure* (inference here that government requests are illegal and unreasonable) *that they are legal and reasonable in scope.*

We urge the US to take the lead and make reforms that ensure that government surveillance efforts are clearly restricted by law, proportionate to the risks, transparent and subject to independent oversight. To see the full set of principles we support, visit ReformGovernmentSurveillance.com

Sincerely,

AOL, Apple, Facebook, Google, LinkedIn, Microsoft, Twitter, Yahoo

As you can see, I'm not a fan of poorly written open letters from executives who did not take the time or effort to create a worthwhile product. This letter seems to be a hurried, gut-reaction to public opinion.

The analysis shows you what you can decipher from letters. Looking at why just one word was used over another can help you determine the motivation, the real purpose for a letter.

While the letter is directed at the US Government, it is really directed to all governments. So, it is confusing from the very beginning. Rather than asking for a "solution," they ask for a *"change."* The word *"change"* is important. Why? *"Change"* is not a "solution." Change has a more temporary feel to it. Solution seems more permanent. Certainly, these executives want something more than fleeting. Change can be due to happenstance. Solution is much more premeditated, more inputs, more thought out. So, why use *"change"* instead of the seemingly more desirable word "solution?" *"Change"* reveals the writers' desire to quickly *"reform government surveillance practices worldwide."* To this extent, this letter is self-serving, to show the writers have an apparent concern while seeking to promote simply, *"a change."* If their thoughts on this were well developed, they would have used the word, "solution." They refer to their *"full set of principles we support,"* which seems to be the beginning of a "solution" but they don't use that word. Since they don't use that word, we can only conclude the real purpose for this letter is not *"reform"* as they state, but to improve the public's perception of them. As evidence of this, note the self-serving second paragraph. "For our part, we are focused on keeping users' data secure — deploying the latest encryption technology to prevent unauthorized surveillance on our networks and by pushing back on government requests to ensure that they are legal and reasonable in scope."

Make no mistake — this "Open Letter to Washington" is a "smoke screen."

13C
THE RAMSAY LETTER

On December 26, 1996, at 5:25 AM Patsy Ramsay called 911 to report her six-year old daughter JonBenét Ramsay as missing and also reported the existence of a ransom note. Several hours later that day at 1:05 PM, John Ramsay found JonBenét 's body in the basement of their home. Her body showed evidence of a fractured skull and strangulation.

The actual letter

ATTACHMENT A

Mr. Ramsey,

Listen carefully! We are a group of individuals that represent a small foreign faction. We do respect your bussiness but not the country that it serves. At this time we have your daughter in our posession. She is safe and unharmed and if you want her to see 1997, you must follow our instructions to the letter.

You will withdraw $118,000.00 from your account. $100,000 will be in $100 bills and the remaining $18,000 in $20 bills. Make sure that you bring an adequate size attache to the bank. When you get home you will put the money in a brown paper bag. I will call you between 8 and 10 am tomorrow to instruct you on delivery. The delivery will be exhausting so I advise you to be rested. If we monitor you getting the money early, we might call you early to arrange an earlier delivery of the

money and hence ~~d~~ earlier
~~delivery~~ pick-up of your daughter.
Any deviation of my instructions
will result in the immediate
execution of your daughter. You
will also be denied her remains
for proper burial. The two
gentlemen watching over your daughter
do not particularly like you so I
advise you not to provoke them.
Speaking to anyone about your
situation, such as Police, F.B.I., etc.,
will result in your daughter being
beheaded. If we catch you talking
to a stray dog, she dies. If you
alert bank authorities, she dies.
If ~~the~~ money is in any way
marked or tampered with, she
dies. You will be scanned for
electronic devices and if any are
found, she dies. You can try to
deceive us but be warned that
we are familiar with law enforcement
countermeasures and tactics. You
stand a 99% chance of killing
your daughter if you try to out
smart us. Follow our instructions

and you stand a 100% chance
of getting her back. You and
your family are under constant
scrutiny as well as the authorities.
Don't try to grow a brain
John. You are not the only
fat cat around so don't think
that killing will be difficult.
Don't underestimate us John.
Use that good southern common
sense of yours. It is up to
you now John!

Victory!

S.B.T.C

My typed version (with line numbers):
My line by line, word by word, analysis (my analysis in bold)
follows. Note all the pronouns and any other like words are
highlighted. A ≠ indicates a missing pronoun.

First of all, the letter is handwritten. This is not unusual.
Kidnappers apparently find it to be necessary. It's old, but
the Lindbergh case comes to mind. We can assume that the
kidnappers felt there was no other viable option. That, alone,
tells us much about the kidnappers. Handwritten ransom notes
leave much evidence: handwriting, finger-prints, DNA, and a host
of other evidence. Suffice it to say this homicide would appear
not to be well planned.

GETTING THE TRUTH

The first thing we can say is that we know one person wrote this note since it's in the same handwriting. A note written by a group of individuals is more difficult to analyze.

We can also note that this was a false note, a note designed to deflect the investigators from would-be suspects. We know that because the autopsy showed JonBenét died before Patsy Ramsay found this note and reported it. The investigation also showed the note paper came from the Ramsay house. Police obtained writing samples from all the Ramsays. They couldn't eliminate Patsy.

My intent for the analysis that follows is to show you what you can do to get the truth. Other experts have done extensive analysis of this note. I simply refer you to those works for a different and more enlightening review. My analysis is unique, however. The following will be based only on what the note said, with little regard as to the facts uncovered in the investigation. While some facts of the case are referred to, most of my analysis will be isolated on the words and sentence structure in the note. With that in mind, here we go.

According to reports, John Ramsay found JonBenét dead at 1:05 PM on 12/26/1996, in the basement of the house. The autopsy report indicates the time of death was from 10 PM on 12/25/1996 to 6 AM on 12/26/1996, likely to be closer to midnight. Patsy Ramsay's call to 911 was at 5:25 AM on 12/26/1996 where she indicated she just found the ransom note. So, the first question we need to answer is why? Why is this a false note? There is no other conclusion.

The note attempts to lead the reader to believe it is the product of a "We are a *group of individuals that represent a small foreign faction."* Note that *"represent"* is not plural. An uneducated person might make that "represents," because of "group." However, the verb relates to "We," and therefore, the singular is correct. This is evidence we have an educated writer. There are what appear to be "intentional" mistakes to "dumb down" this letter. There are what appear to be intentional misspellings and references (all detailed in the analysis that follows) that appear to be an attempt to "dumb down" the letter. In the note, the writer, who is careful to use the inclusive pronouns "we" and "our" switches to the singular pronoun "I" and "my" in the middle portions of the note. In these "I" and "my" portions, the writer reveals his/her personal possession or responsibility for the note's contents and directives. These pronoun changes are critical to understanding and possibly identifying the writer.

So, our specific intent in this analysis is to identify the writer, or develop some evidence that will help identify the writer.

The timeline of events (from the initial phone call to a few days following discovery of the body) is important to understand this analysis:

A brief timeline of the JonBenét Ramsey case:

The Denver Post
Oct. 14, 1999
Wednesday, Dec. 25, 1996
The last time JonBenét's parents, John and Patsy Ramsey, say they saw their 6-year-old daughter alive. JonBenét heads to bed at the family home in Boulder's exclusive Chautauqua neighborhood. In addition to her parents, JonBenét's 9-year-old brother, Burke, is at the home that night.

Thursday, Dec. 26, 1996

Patsy Ramsey gets up to make coffee around 5:30 a.m. and reports finding a 2 1/2-page note on a back staircase of the house. The note says JonBenét has been kidnapped and demands $118,000 in cash. The Ramseys call police, who begin an investigation into what they believe is a kidnapping. That afternoon, John Ramsey searches the home and discovers JonBenét's body in a spare room in the basement that was used to hide Christmas presents. She had been strangled with a garrote, and her mouth and neck had been bound with duct tape. At 10:45 p.m. the Boulder County coroner's staff removes JonBenét's body from the house.

1ˈ Mr. Ramsay,

2

3   Listen carefully! We are a
4 group of individuals that represent
5 a small foreign faction. We ~~xx~~
6 respect your bussiness but not the
7 country that it serves. At this
8 time we have your daughter in our
9 posession. She is safe and unharmed
10 and if you want her to see 1997,
11 you must follow our instructions to
12 the letter.
13   You will withdraw $118,000.00
14 from your account. $100,000 will be
15 in $100 bills and the remaining
16 $18,000 in $20 bills. ≠Make sure
17 that you bring an adequate size
18 attache to the bank. When you
19 get home you will put the money
20 in a brown paper bag. I will
21 call you between 8 and 10 am
22 tomorrow to instruct you on delivery.
23 The delivery will be exhausting so
24 I advise you to be rested. If
25 we monitor you getting the money
26 early, we might call you early to
27 arrange an earlier delivery of the
28 money and hence a earlier
29 ~~delivery~~ pickup of your daughter.

30

31   Any deviation of my instructions
32 will result in the immediate
33 execution of your daughter. You
34 will also be denied her remains
35 for proper burial. The two
36 gentlemen watching over your daughter
37 do **not** particularly like you so I
38 advise you not to provoke them.

GETTING THE TRUTH

```
39   ≠Speaking to anyone about your
40   situation, such as Police, F.B.I., etc.,
41   will result in your daughter being
42   beheaded. If we catch you talking
43   to a stray dog, she dies. If you
44   alert bank authorities, she dies.
45   If the money is in any way
46   marked or tampered with, she
47   dies. You will be scanned for
48   electronic devices and if any are
49   found, she dies. You can try to
50   deceive us but be warned that
51   we are familiar with Law enforcement
52   countermeasures and tactics. You
53   stand a 99% chance of killing
54   your daughter if you try to out
55   smart us. ≠Follow our instructions
56   and you stand a 100% chance
57   of getting her back. You and
58   your family are under constant
59   scrutiny as well as the authorities.
60   ≠Don't try to grow a brain
61   John. You are not the only
62   fat cat around so ≠don't think
63   that killing ≠ will be difficult.
64   ≠Don't underestimate us John.
65   ≠Use that good southern common
66   sense of yours. It is up to
67   you now John!
68
69                          Victory!
70                          S.B.T.C
```

Line 1: This is directed to Mr. Ramsay, not Mrs. Ramsay.

Lines 3 — 9: Note the exclamation mark! My experience tells me the odds are better that a female uses an exclamation mark than a male. There is another exclamation mark at the sign off on the letter, Victory! Watch the pronouns, where they are missing and where they change. Why are the sentences *"We are a group of individuals that represent a small foreign faction. We ~~do~~ respect your bussiness (sic) but not the country that it serves,"* here? They are written first, so we must assume they are very important to the writer(s). That which is first is always important. Why? It's the start. It's the beginning. The beginning sets the tone and direction for all to follow. If nothing follows to support the beginning, then we must assume the beginning is unimportant, which defies logic. It means there was no purpose in putting it there in the first place. There is no support for these opening statements in the remaining portion of the letter. Simply put, this beginning makes no sense. We must conclude this beginning was designed to deceive, to deflect. And, we have to ask ourselves who would benefit from that strategy?

The phrase, *"We ~~do~~ respect your bussiness (sic) but not the country it serves,"* appears strange. How many of us think of our businesses as serving their country? John Ramsay's company is a computer graphics company and a subsidiary of Lockheed Martin, a company that holds many U.S. Government contracts. So, at first glance the phrase seems strange, but knowing the fact that John Ramsay's company may hold U.S. Government contracts provides some light. This tells me the person who wrote this is aware that his company works with the government. But, again, why state this — especially at the beginning? My interpretation of all this is the only logical explanation to this inconsistency is if the beginning is not true. And, if the beginning is not true, then again, we need to ask ourselves why? Why is there deception at the beginning? Kidnappers need to establish credibility early, leaving little to doubt. Why start with doubt? We know the note is an instrument of deflection, of deception, now we know the writer has knowledge about John Ramsay's business.

Cross outs are notable because they give us a glimpse into what the writer is thinking. In this case, the writer started to write *"We do ~~not~~ respect."* What was she/he going to write? Also, note the misspelling of "bussiness" and later "posession." There are no other misspellings in the letter(maybe "scrutiny," on the last page), far more difficult to spell words like "authorities," "tomorrow," "deviation," "counter measures," "attache," etc. Also, these two misspelled words are close together — as if to emphasize. Furthermore, and again, they appear at the beginning of the letter and that is done for a purpose. It's important for the writer to make sure we see those. Because of that, and the earlier determination this is an educated writer, it is quite probable these misspellings are intentional.

"At this time we have your daughter in our posession (sic)." This is a verbose way of saying, "We have your daughter." Verbosity is artillery (referred to in Chapter 5). Why the need to convince that they have her? The Ramsay's shouldn't need convincing that they have her because she is nowhere to be found. Why spend extra time and effort on something that should be a known? The kidnappers would know where she is. Why the *"At this time,"* and why the need to say, *"in our posession* (sic)?" Was it so the writer(s) could include another misspelling? Also, *"At this time"* connotes something temporary, not permanent. This could have been written, simply, "We have your daughter," but the writer

chose not to say that. Why? This does not promote the certainty, continuity of having his daughter. This is another sign this is not a legitimate note.

Let's also look at the sentence, *"She is safe and unharmed and if you want her to see 1997, you must follow our instructions to the letter."* This could have been said much more simply: "If you want her to see 1997, you must follow our instructions." Again, the writer(s) style is unnecessarily wordy. Why not, "if you want to see her?" Isn't that sufficient? We must infer the writer has a need to be specific. This is an area that would be of interest to me if I were to examine writing samples from suspected writers of the note. The phrase, "to the letter," is unnecessary also, almost legalistic.

On almost every word, every phrase, I ask the question, why? Why would the writer intentionally misspell words and include unnecessary information? Again, kidnappers rely on the unknown and the impressions they leave on the would-be victims and they need to quickly establish credibility. They want the would-be victims to believe they are serious, cunning, strategic, disciplined, and determined. So far, the inclusion of unnecessary information and the apparent intentional inclusion of misspellings create the wrong impressions. That is inconsistent and suspicious.

Lines 13 — 55: So, the $118,000 figure is certainly a curious amount. Why not a round figure of say, $1,000,000? These are wealthy would-be victims and *"a group of individuals that represent a small foreign faction,"* would certainly ask for more than $118,000 wouldn't you think? Also, we suspect the writer knows John's business, and therefore, would know his wealth. This low, insignificant $118,000, again, defies logic. Things that defy logic are usually illogical.

More important analysis here takes place when looking at lines 20 - 24. What do you see here? You should see the shifting of the writer's pronouns. The pronouns up to this point are "we," and, "our." Now we see, line 20, *"I will call you between 8 and 10 am (note the "am" is not capitalized) tomorrow to instruct you on delivery. The delivery will be exhausting so I advise you to be rested."* Now a shift back, *"If we monitor..."* The writer now reveals himself or herself to be the one who will call tomorrow. So, if John Ramsay should receive a call *"tomorrow,"* we are led to believe the caller will be the writer of this note. The shift in pronouns was unnecessary. There would be no change in meaning if the note read, " in a brown paper bag. We will call you between 8 and 10 am tomorrow to instruct you on delivery. The delivery will be exhausting so we advise you to be rested." Unnecessary changes alert us to important changes. So, why the change? The change now makes the note personal. Up to now, the writer was writing for the "group," for the "faction." Now, the writer becomes personally involved and inserts himself or herself directly into this note. That shows a level of emotion that wasn't revealed before. This tells me there is more to this note than the stated reason, "$118,000.00" It's now personal. So, now we know the writer has a personal interest, and that's telling.

The word *"tomorrow"* is of particular interest. Since we know the note is a fake, the writer most likely wrote this note on 12/25/1996, which is consistent with what we now know to be the time of death. Patsy Ramsay states in the 911 call, "... a note was left." She later advised she found the note on their staircase. What if Patsy woke up at 0900 or 1000? This adds further to the importance that the writer had inside knowledge, knowing the family wakes up long before the kidnapper's call would come in. Also, when is "tomorrow." Is tomorrow the day after the note is found (which is kind of indeterminate) or is it the day after the note was written? How can the reader interpret that? How are the Ramsay's to know when or what *"tomorrow"* is? Again, this is illogical and another indication this note is a fake. Patsy Ramsay had a BA in Journalism, graduating magna cum laude. John Ramsay had a bachelor's degree in Electrical Engineering and a Master's Degree from Michigan State University. Could either of these two write this letter?

Let's also look at line 31, "Any deviation of my instructions," and line 55: ". . . follow our instructions." One minute these are "my instructions," the next minute they are "our instructions." This is another inconsistency.

What do these pronoun changes mean? In the first pronoun switch, line 20, *"I will call you . . ."* is logical. *The second in line 24, ". . . I advise you to be rested,"* is illogical. It would seem a *"we"* in lieu of the "I" would have been more consistent. These pronoun changes are not a mistake. They are there because the writer got caught up in the story and wrote what he/she thought would be reasonable in a kidnapper's note. In line 37, " the pronoun "I" in the sentence starting at line 24 also provides us greater insight: `". . . so I advise you not to provoke them."` This is especially enlightening because it infers the writer has no control over his/her associates. That seems not to be credible since the writer is the one poviding the instructions and calling the shots. Yet again, another point which shows this to be a false note and a writer who is lacking "street" sense.

```
"If
we monitor you getting the money
early, we might call you early to
arrange an earlier delivery of the
money and a earlier
delivery pickup of your daughter."
```

It's unlikely that a kidnapper's note would include a contingency plan like this one. "If we monitor you getting the money early, we might call you early . . . ?" The word, "hence" is particularly interesting in that it is unusual — very unusual. When is the last time you used the word, "hence?" Kidnappers would be unlikely to use that word. It's more likely a term used by a woman than a man. This is another point of focus when looking at writing samples to help identify the writer.

Let's also look at all the instances of missing pronouns: lines 3, 14, 16, 38, 55, 60, 62, 63, 64, 65. Missing pronouns are those pronouns that the writer chose not to use, even though a pronoun could have been used. Here are the sentences where the pronoun is missing:

3.   Listen carefully.
14. ≠ $100,000 will be in....
16. ≠ Make sure that you
39. ≠ Speaking to anyone
55. ≠ Follow our instructions
60. ≠ Don't try to grow
62. ≠ Don't think that
63. ≠ that killing xx will be difficult
64. ≠ Don't underestimate us
65. ≠ Use that good southern

Note the *"killing will be difficult."* Killing who? It's reasonable to assume the missing pronoun is the daughter. This is an important missing pronoun. Was the writer unable to write "her," " your daughter," or "JonBenét ?" The full line is, *"You are not the only fat cat around so don't think that killing will be difficult."* The *"fat cat,"* verbiage seems to be out of context. Moreover, this is American slang, not foreign. It has to do with having money, not being able to kill. It shows the writer's naiveté. Also, it just doesn't fit the context. What does a "fat cat" have to do with being able to kill? This may be another sign the writer is a female. There is "street knowledge" lacking in the writer's thought process.

Six of the 10 missing pronouns appear in the last 11 lines of the note. Why? Was the writer in a hurry?

Let's also look at where the writer uses contractions. As discussed earlier, contractions are used when the writer feels less stress, more confidence, and more comfort. In this note, there are only three contractions, and they all appear in the last six lines of the note: (lines 60, 62, and 64)

```
"≠Don't try to grow a brain
John. You are not the only
fat cat around so ≠don't think
that killing ≠ will be difficult.
≠Don't underestimate us John.
≠Use that good southern common
sense of yours. It is up to
you now John!"
```

So, the writer pushes a relatively large percentage of his/ her missing pronouns and contractions into the last few lines of the note. Again, does that tell us anything? I believe it does. It all points to the writer wrapping up the note in a hurried way to finish it. There is an exhalation; a relief the note is just about finished. Also note that John is not southern, but Patsy is.

Conclusion:

Let's just get to the point. No surprise here. The identity of the writer lies in the language used, the words used (hence?), the intentional misspellings, the pronoun change from plural to personal pronouns revealing the writer to have a personal interest, the female aspects of the words, phrases, and emotions used, where the writer placed the misspellings, the exclamation marks, the apparent lack of street sense, the hurried manner in which the note is written. The writer was likely Patsy Ramsay.

13D
THE DAVID PETRAEUS LETTER
9 NOVEMBER 2012

HEADQUARTERS

Central Intelligence Agency   used, employed, exercised

9 November 2012

Yesterday afternoon, I went to the White House and asked
the President to be allowed, for personal reasons, to
resign from my position as D/CIA. After being married
for over 37 years, I showed extremely poor judgment by
engaging in an extramarital affair. Such behavior is
unacceptable, both as a husband and as the leader of an
organization such as ours. This afternoon, the President
graciously accepted my resignation.

          becoming involved, participating

As I depart Langley, I want you to know that it has been
the greatest of privileges to have served with you, the
officers of our Nation's Silent Service, a work force
that is truly exceptional in every regard. Indeed, you
did extraordinary work on a host of critical missions
during my time as director, and I am deeply grateful to
you for that.

Teddy Roosevelt once observed that life's greatest gift
is the opportunity to work hard at work worth doing. I
will always treasure my opportunity to have done that
with you and I will always regret the circumstances that
brought that work with you to an end.

Thank you for your extraordinary service to our country,
and best wishes for continued success in the important
endeavors that lie ahead for our country and our Agency.

With admiration and appreciation,

David H. Petraeus

GETTING THE TRUTH

This is David Petraeus' letter to colleagues following his resignation as Director of the CIA due to his admittedly inappropriate relationship with Paula Broadwell. At first glance I note the large number of the personal pronoun "I." This shows his ability for personal commitment and responsibility. However, we need to put all that in context. I also note there is no reference to a "decision or decisions," which I would expect. After all, bad decisions led to his resignation. To understand further, let's look more closely.

"I went to the White House," starts out as a good sentence in that it starts with an "I," showing personal commitment and accountability and contains the past tense verb "went," which makes me believe he did go to the White House.

This will be a good example to study how Alvin (Chapter 4) conducts his very subtle and elaborate artwork. Look not only at what is said, but how it is said, how it is not said, and where in the statement it is said. Ask why is it said that way? Is everything there you would expect to be there? What is missing? What is there that shouldn't be there? Were there any words you would expect to be there, that aren't?

Petraeus "Yesterday, I went to the White House and asked the President to be allowed, for personal reasons, to resign from my position as D/CIA."

This could have been stated in a much simpler way: "Yesterday, I asked the President to allow me, for personal reasons, to resign as D/CIA." Note the difference in physical distance between Petraeus and the President in Petraeus' version and mine. Petraeus' version shows much greater distance between the two. The *"personal reasons"* portion may be unnecessary, but let's just assume he wants to make it clear he didn't offer his resignation for professional reasons. The unnecessarily added physical distance in the original sentence structure between himself and the President is an indication he dislikes the President.

Further, Petraeus' verbiage and sentence structure in that opening sentence puts further distance between the <u>President</u> and the decision *"to be allowed to resign."* Note, in my more simpler version, my wording is *"to allow me to resign."* The added distance and more passive voice verbiage in the original sentence are important. That distance and the verbiage diminish the President's role in that resignation. In my version, the President either allows or doesn't allow my resignation; in the original ("to be allowed"), the President's role is murkier, cloudier, more vague, more removed, suggesting the decision was more Petraeus' than the President's. This may be Petraeus' way to preserve his ego. But, it also adds evidence to my earlier conclusion that he dislikes the President.

His next sentence, *"... I showed extremely poor judgment by engaging in an extramarital affair,"* contains words that need exploration. The word, *"showed,"* reveals Petraeus as less reticent than he would like us to believe. He could have said, "used, employed, exercised" in place of "showed." The use of those words would better reflect his poor decisions, and faulty thought process. Whereas, the word "showed" tells us his thinking at the time this letter was written and it reveals a more superficial, almost unemotional depiction of a man who was caught *showing "extremely poor judgment,"* as opposed to a man <u>acting</u> on extremely poor judgment. "Showing," carries less accountability than "acting," or "using" or "exercising."

His use of the word, "*engaging in an extramarital affair,*" shows a much higher emotional level than had he used the words," by becoming involved in an extramarital affair, or by participating in an extramarital affair." The word, "engaging" reveals Petraeus' involvement was not just a physical affair, but an emotional one as well. And, of course, his use of the word, "affair," confirms this finding. He could have called it "extramarital activities," or "extramarital involvement," or "extramarital matters." The word "affair" carries further emotional characteristics that the other words don't.

The next notable phrase is in the following paragraph: "*As I depart Langley, I want you to know that it has been the greatest of privileges to have served with you, the officers of our Nation's Silent Service, a work force that is truly exceptional in every regard. Indeed, you did extraordinary work on a host of critical missions during my time as director, and I am deeply grateful to you for that.*" I will leave other words in this letter for you to review, analyze, and consider to help you test your skills. The phrase I want to concentrate on in this passage is the "*for that.*" This is a form of a qualifier. Qualifiers tell the reader that while the writer is happy for what preceded the, "for that," the writer is not happy with something else. The sentence would have been much more complimentary had it read, "*As I depart Langley, I want you to know that it has been the greatest of privileges to have served with you, the officers of our Nation's Silent Service, a work force that is truly exceptional in every regard. Indeed, you did extraordinary work on a host of critical missions during my time as director, and I am deeply grateful to you.*" The only reason for the "for that," is to reveal he is displeased with something else the officers of the Nation's Silent Service did or didn't do.

In the next paragraph, *"Teddy Roosevelt once observed that life's greatest gift is the opportunity to work hard at work worth doing. I will always treasure my opportunity to have done that with you and I will always regret the* circumstances *that brought that work with you to an end."* "Circumstances" is a curious word here. The word "circumstances" has a "blameless" connotation to it. "Circumstances beyond my control," comes to mind. So, the "circumstances brought that work with you to an end," not his actions. A statement that read, ". . . and I will always regret the poor decisions I made that brought that work with you to an end" would seem to more appropriate for someone who was truly reticent and remorseful. After all, that was what occurred. This sentence, along with the earlier analysis, reads to mean he regrets getting caught, which is the real message that this letter exudes.

13E
THE DYLAN FARROW OPEN LETTER
FEBRUARY 1, 2014

Let's take a look at Dylan Farrow's open letter concerning her 1993 accusation that her adoptive father, famed actor, writer, and comedian Woody Allen, sexually abused her when she was seven years old. Her letter was published on February 1, 2014:

Dylan Farrow Open Letter:

GETTING THE TRUTH

1   What's your favorite Woody Allen movie?
2   Before you answer, you should know: when I
3   was seven years old, Woody Allen took me by
4   the hand and led me into a dim, closet-like
5   attic on the second floor of our house. He
6   told me to lay on my stomach and play with my
7   brother's electric train set. Then he
8   sexually assaulted me. He talked to me while
9   he did it, whispering that I was a good girl,
10   that this was our secret, promising that we'd
11   go to Paris and I'd be a star in his movies.
12   I remember staring at that toy train,
13   focusing on it as it traveled in its circle
14   around the attic. To this day, I find it
15   difficult to look at toy trains.

16   For as long as I could remember, my father
17   had been doing things to me that I didn't
18   like. I didn't like how often he would take
19   me away from my mom, siblings and friends to
20   be alone with him. I didn't like it when he
21   would stick his thumb in my mouth. I didn't
22   like it when I had to get in bed with him
23   under the sheets when he was in his underwear.
24   I didn't like it when he would place his head
25   in my naked lap and breathe in and breathe
26   out. I would hide under beds or lock myself
27   in the bathroom to avoid these encounters,
28   but he always found me. These things happened
29   so often, so routinely, so skillfully hidden
30   from a mother that would have protected me
31   had she known, that I thought it was normal.
32   I thought this was how fathers doted on their
33   daughters. But what he did to me in the attic
34   felt different. I couldn't keep the secret
35   anymore.

36   When I asked my mother if her dad did to her
37   what Woody Allen did to me, I honestly did
38   not know the answer. I also didn't know the

39 firestorm it would trigger. I didn't know
40 that my father would use his sexual
41 relationship with my sister to cover up the
42 abuse he inflicted on me. I didn't know that
43 he would accuse my mother of planting the
44 abuse in my head and call her a liar for
45 defending me. I didn't know that I would be
46 made to recount my story over and over again,
47 to doctor after doctor, pushed to see if I'd
48 admit I was lying as part of a legal battle I
49 couldn't possibly understand. At one point,
50 my mother sat me down and told me that I
51 wouldn't be in trouble if I was lying — that
52 I could take it all back. I couldn't. It was
53 all true. But sexual abuse claims against the
54 powerful stall more easily. There were
55 experts willing to attack my credibility.
56 There were doctors willing to gaslight an
57 abused child.

58 After a custody hearing denied my father
59 visitation rights, my mother declined to
60 pursue criminal charges, despite findings of
61 probable cause by the State of Connecticut —
62 due to, in the words of the prosecutor, the
63 fragility of the "child victim." Woody Allen
64 was never convicted of any crime. That he got
65 away with what he did to me haunted me as I
66 grew up. I was stricken with guilt that I had
67 allowed him to be near other little girls. I
68 was terrified of being touched by men. I
69 developed an eating disorder. I began cutting
70 myself. That torment was made worse by
71 Hollywood. All but a precious few (my heroes)
72 turned a blind eye. Most found it easier to
73 accept the ambiguity, to say, "who can say
74 what happened," to pretend that nothing was
75 wrong. Actors praised him at awards shows.
76 Networks put him on TV. Critics put him in
77 magazines. Each time I saw my abuser's face —

78 on a poster, on a t-shirt, on television — I
79 could only hide my panic until I found a
80 place to be alone and fall apart.

81 Last week, Woody Allen was nominated for his
82 latest Oscar. But this time, I refuse to fall
83 apart. For so long, Woody Allen's acceptance
84 silenced me. It felt like a personal rebuke,
85 like the awards and accolades were a way to
86 tell me to shut up and go away. But the
87 survivors of sexual abuse who have reached
88 out to me — to support me and to share their
89 fears of coming forward, of being called a
90 liar, of being told their memories aren't
91 their memories — have given me a reason to
92 not be silent, if only so others know that
93 they don't have to be silent either.
94 Today, I consider myself lucky. I am happily
95 married. I have the support of my amazing
96 brothers and sisters. I have a mother who
97 found within herself a well of fortitude that
98 saved us from the chaos a predator brought
99 into our home.

100 But others are still scared, vulnerable, and
101 struggling for the courage to tell the truth.
102 The message that Hollywood sends matters for
103 them.

104 What if it had been your child, Cate
105 Blanchett? Louis CK? Alec Baldwin? What if it
106 had been you, Emma Stone? Or you, Scarlett
107 Johansson? You knew me when I was a little
108 girl, Diane Keaton. Have you forgotten me?

109 Woody Allen is a living testament to the way
110 our society fails the survivors of sexual
111 assault and abuse.

112   So imagine your seven-year-old daughter being
113   led into an attic by Woody Allen. Imagine she
114   spends a lifetime stricken with nausea at the
115   mention of his name. Imagine a world that
116   celebrates her tormenter.

117   Are you imagining that? Now, what's your
118   favorite Woody Allen movie?

**Legend for the highlights in my analysis
of Dylan Farrow's letter:**

Actor and/or Important Descriptors

Pronouns and substitutes

Significant Descriptors

GETTING THE TRUTH

1   What's your favorite Woody Allen movie?

2   Before you answer, you should know: when I

3   was seven years old, Woody Allen took me by

4   the hand and led me into a dim, closet-like

5   attic on the second floor of our house. He

6   told me to lay on my stomach and play with my

7   brother's electric train set. Then he

8   sexually assaulted me. He talked to me while

9   he did it, whispering that I was a good girl,

10   that this was our secret, promising that we'd

11   go to Paris and I'd be a star in his movies.

12   I remember staring at that toy train,

13   focusing on it as it traveled in its circle

14   around the attic. To this day, I find it

15   difficult to look at toy trains.

16   For as long as I could remember, my father

17   had been doing things to me that I didn't

18   like. I didn't like how often he would take

19   me away from my mom, siblings and friends to

20   be alone with him. I didn't like it when he

21   would stick his thumb in my mouth. I didn't

22   like it when I had to get in bed with him

23   under the sheets when he was in his underwear.

24   I didn't like it when he would place his head

25   in my naked lap and breathe in and breathe

26   out. I would hide under beds or lock myself

27   in the bathroom to avoid these encounters,

28 but he always found me. These things happened
29 so often, so routinely, so skillfully hidden
30 from a mother that would have protected me
31 had she known, that I thought it was normal.
32 I thought this was how fathers doted on their
33 daughters. But what he did to me in the attic
34 felt different. I couldn't keep the secret
35 anymore.
36 When I asked my mother if her dad did to her
37 what Woody Allen did to me, I honestly did
38 not know the answer. I also didn't know the
39 firestorm it would trigger. I didn't know
40 that my father would use his sexual
41 relationship with my sister to cover up the
42 abuse he inflicted on me. I didn't know that
43 he would accuse my mother of planting the
44 abuse in my head and call her a liar for
45 defending me. I didn't know that I would be
46 made to recount my story over and over again,
47 to doctor after doctor, pushed to see if I'd
48 admit I was lying as part of a legal battle I
49 couldn't possibly understand. At one point,
50 my mother sat me down and told me that I
51 wouldn't be in trouble if I was lying — that
52 I could take it all back. I couldn't. It was
53 all true. But sexual abuse claims against the
54 powerful stall more easily. There were

55 experts willing to attack my credibility.

56 There were doctors willing to gaslight an

57 abused child.

58 After a custody hearing denied my father

59 visitation rights, my mother declined to

60 pursue criminal charges, despite findings of

61 probable cause by the State of Connecticut —

62 due to, in the words of the prosecutor, the

63 fragility of the "child victim." Woody Allen

64 was never convicted of any crime. That he got

65 away with what he did to me haunted me as I

66 grew up. I was stricken with guilt that I had

67 allowed him to be near other little girls. I

68 was terrified of being touched by men. I

69 developed an eating disorder. I began cutting

70 myself. That torment was made worse by

71 Hollywood. All but a precious few (my heroes)

72 turned a blind eye. Most found it easier to

73 accept the ambiguity, to say, "who can say

74 what happened," to pretend that nothing was

75 wrong. Actors praised him at awards shows.

76 Networks put him on TV. Critics put him in

77 magazines. Each time I saw my abuser's face —

78 on a poster, on a t-shirt, on television — I

79 could only hide my panic until I found a

80 place to be alone and fall apart.

81 Last week, Woody Allen was nominated for his

82 latest Oscar. But this time, I refuse to fall
83 apart. For so long, Woody Allen's acceptance
84 silenced me. It felt like a personal rebuke,
85 like the awards and accolades were a way to
86 tell me to shut up and go away. But the
87 survivors of sexual abuse who have reached
88 out to me — to support me and to share their
89 fears of coming forward, of being called a
90 liar, of being told their memories aren't
91 their memories — have given me a reason to
92 not be silent, if only so others know that
93 they don't have to be silent either.
94 Today, I consider myself lucky. I am happily
95 married. I have the support of my amazing
96 brothers and sisters. I have a mother who
97 found within herself a well of fortitude that
98 saved us from the chaos a predator brought
99 into our home.
100 But others are still scared, vulnerable, and
101 struggling for the courage to tell the truth.
102 The message that Hollywood sends matters for
103 them.
104 What if it had been your child, Cate
105 Blanchett? Louis CK? Alec Baldwin? What if it
106 had been you, Emma Stone? Or you, Scarlett
107 Johansson? You knew me when I was a little
108 girl, Diane Keaton. Have you forgotten me?
109 Woody Allen is a living testament to the way

110 our society fails the survivors of sexual

111 assault and abuse.

112 So imagine your seven-year-old daughter being

113 led into an attic by Woody Allen. Imagine she

114 spends a lifetime stricken with nausea at the

115 mention of his name. Imagine a world that

116 celebrates her tormentor.

117 Are you imagining that? Now, what's your

118 favorite Woody Allen movie?

**Legend for the highlights in my analysis
of Dylan Farrow's letter:**

Actor and/or Important Descriptors

Pronouns and substitutes

Significant Descriptors

When analyzing past events, I always highlight the pronouns, personal pronouns, and look at the voice, whether it's active or passive. I like to see the first person pronoun, "I," because, when used, it connotes personal commitment. The "I" coupled with a past tense verb in the active voice is a powerful sign that the statement is truthful. Ms. Farrow's coupling of the first person pronoun with a past tense verb is consistent throughout the letter. This is strong evidence of truthfulness.

I also look for changes in voice. Changes in voice have to be explained or found logical. I see no voice changes after the opening, "when I was seven years old," that concern me.

I look for flow, to see if the thoughts are completed, and words are as expected or easily understood. I look for logic and consistency. I also look for missing information. The thought flow in this letter is very good, with the first and last sentences pulling it all together. I see no unexpected words or words that seem out of place or inexplicable. Following review and analysis, I have no concerns in these areas.

Next, I put boxes around key people, words, descriptive phrases, and noteworthy language. The first and last sentences wrap up the statement. They prepare and conclude what falls in between. I draw lines to connect the labels for the main actor and key words or phrases.

She starts labeling the main actor of her statement, "Woody Allen," (9 times) then refers to him as "my father," (3) then, "my abuser," (1) then, "a predator," (1,), her "tormentor," (1). Let's see if these label changes make sense. I want to know if her "my father," labels are justified or seem reasonable given her apparent high degree of mental pain and aguish. Yes, he is her father, but the personal pronoun "my," is a special one. "My," connotes closeness, affection, and ownership. I wouldn't expect her to repeatedly call him "my father." Victims don't refer to their assaulters in ways that reflect affection or close affiliation. Such language would be inconsistent and might be indicative of deception or a false report. Let's see if analysis shows her labels to be reasonable, logical. The 3 "my fathers" appear on lines 16, 40, and 58.

There are no "my fathers," past line 58 of a 118 line statement. The first appears on line 16 at the beginning of a paragraph that follows the paragraph where she refers to him as "Woody Allen" and describes the sexual assault. So, there is separation from the main sexual assault allegation that occurs in the attic when she was seven years old. This "my father" occurs on line 16, at the beginning of the paragraph. "For as long as I could remember, my father had been doing things to me that I didn't like." She, thus, can refer to him as "my father" when "had been doing things to me that I didn't like," but does not refer to him as "my father" for the sexual assault. I can accept that.

The second reference to "my father" shows in line 40: "I didn't know that my father would use his sexual relationship with my sister to cover up the abuses he inflicted on me." This "my father" label is used to describe a strategy, not a specific sexual act, so this is logical and reasonable.

The third reference, line 58, at the beginning of a new paragraph: "After a custody hearing denied my father visitation rights, . . ." This reference is logical and reasonable.

Let's look at the contexts in which she used the labels "Woody Allen," "my abuser," "a predator." "Woody Allen" is used in lines 1, 3, 37, 63, 81, 83, 109, 113, and 118.

In the first paragraph, line 3, the "Woody Allen" "<u>sexually assaulted</u> me;" In line 37, "Woody Allen <u>did to me</u>;" Line 63, "Woody Allen was never convicted of any crime." Line 81 ". . . Woody Allen was nominated."; Line 83, ". . . Woody Allen's acceptance <u>silenced me</u>;" Line 109, "Woody Allen is living testament to the way our society fails the survivors of sexual abuse;" Line 113, "So imagine your seven-year-old daughter <u>being led</u> into an attic by Woody Allen." She associates the label Woody Allen with pain, suffering, and social injustice.

Let's look at the descriptive words she uses throughout this statement to see if they are consistent, logical, and reasonable given her allegation. I'll just list the words I've highlighted (with some context): "took me by the hand . . . led me into a dim, closet-like attic . . . told me . . . sexually assaulted me . . . talked to me while he did it . . . whispering that I was a good girl . . . this was our secret . . . promising . . . I remember staring . . . focusing on it . . . doing things to me . . . stick his thumb in my mouth . . . get in bed with him under the sheets . . . he would place his head in my naked lap and breathe in and breathe out . . . I would hide . . . or lock myself in the bathroom . . . to avoid . . . he always found me . . . so skillfully hidden . . . what he did to me in the attic . . . the secret . . . the abuse he inflicted on me . . . he got away with what he did to me . . . I had allowed him to be near other girls . . . Each time I saw my abuser's face . . . hide my panic . . . until I found a place to be alone and fall apart . . . silenced me . . . being called a liar . . . the chaos a predator brought into our home . . . stricken with nausea . . . a world that celebrates her tormentor."

There's really no need for further analysis. This is a truthful statement from a young female victim who has relived her nightmare all too many times. This open letter should serve as a monument to truthful statements. I hope she finds peace.

13F
WOODY ALLEN SPEAKS OUT
By Woody Allen February 7, 2013

Let's now analyze Woody Allen's response to Dylan Farrow's open letter, as it appeared in the New York Times, February 7, 2014. I will give you his response with line numbers, then conduct the analysis of his response in the second section. My conclusions will follow.

```
1   TWENTY-ONE years ago, when I first heard Mia
2   Farrow had accused me of child molestation, I
3   found the idea so ludicrous I didn't give it
4   a second thought. We were involved in a
5   terribly acrimonious breakup, with great
6   enmity between us and a custody battle slowly
7   gathering energy. The self-serving
8   transparency of her malevolence seemed so
9   obvious I didn't even hire a lawyer to defend
10  myself. It was my show business attorney who
11  told me she was bringing the accusation to
12  the police and I would need a criminal lawyer.

13  I naïvely thought the accusation would be
14  dismissed out of hand because of course, I
15  hadn't molested Dylan and any rational person
16  would see the ploy for what it was. Common
17  sense would prevail. After all, I was a 56-
18  year-old man who had never before (or after)
19  been accused of child molestation. I had been
20  going out with Mia for 12 years and never in
21  that time did she ever suggest to me anything
22  resembling misconduct. Now, suddenly, when I
23  had driven up to her house in Connecticut one
24  afternoon to visit the kids for a few hours,
25  when I would be on my raging adversary's home
26  turf, with half a dozen people present, when I
27  was in the blissful early stages of a happy
28  new relationship with the woman I'd go on to
29  marry — that I would pick this moment in time
```

30 to embark on a career as a child molester
31 should seem to the most skeptical mind highly
32 unlikely. The sheer illogic of such a crazy
33 scenario seemed to me dispositive.

34 Notwithstanding, Mia insisted that I had
35 abused Dylan and took her immediately to a
36 doctor to be examined. Dylan told the doctor
37 she had not been molested. Mia then took
38 Dylan out for ice cream, and when she came
39 back with her the child had changed her story.
40 The police began their investigation; a
41 possible indictment hung in the balance. I
42 very willingly took a lie-detector test and
43 of course passed because I had nothing to hide.
44 I asked Mia to take one and she wouldn't.
45 Last week a woman named Stacey Nelkin, whom I
46 had dated many years ago, came forward to the
47 press to tell them that when Mia and I first
48 had our custody battle 21 years ago, Mia had
49 wanted her to testify that she had been
50 underage when I was dating her, despite the
51 fact this was untrue. Stacey refused. I
52 include this anecdote so we all know what kind
53 of character we are dealing with here. One can
54 imagine in learning this why she wouldn't take
55 a lie-detector test.

56 Meanwhile the Connecticut police turned for
57 help to a special investigative unit they
58 relied on in such cases, the Child Sexual
59 Abuse Clinic of the Yale-New Haven Hospital.
60 This group of impartial, experienced men and
61 women whom the district attorney looked to for
62 guidance as to whether to prosecute, spent
63 months doing a meticulous investigation,
64 interviewing everyone concerned, and checking
65 every piece of evidence. Finally they wrote
66 their conclusion which I quote here: "It is
67 our expert opinion that Dylan was not sexually
68 abused by Mr. Allen. Further, we believe that

69 Dylan's statements on videotape and her
70 statements to us during our evaluation do not
71 refer to actual events that occurred to her on
72 August 4th, 1992... In developing our opinion
73 we considered three hypotheses to explain
74 Dylan's statements. First, that Dylan's
75 statements were true and that Mr. Allen had
76 sexually abused her; second, that Dylan's
77 statements were not true but were made up by
78 an emotionally vulnerable child who was caught
79 up in a disturbed family and who was
80 responding to the stresses in the family; and
81 third, that Dylan was coached or influenced by
82 her mother, Ms. Farrow. While we can conclude
83 that Dylan was not sexually abused, we can not
84 be definite about whether the second
85 formulation by itself or the third formulation
86 by itself is true. We believe that it is more
87 likely that a combination of these two
88 formulations best explains Dylan's allegations
89 of sexual abuse."

90 Could it be any clearer? Mr. Allen did not
91 abuse Dylan; most likely a vulnerable,
92 stressed-out 7-year-old was coached by Mia
93 Farrow. This conclusion disappointed a number
94 of people. The district attorney was champing
95 at the bit to prosecute a celebrity case, and
96 Justice Elliott Wilk, the custody judge,
97 wrote a very irresponsible opinion saying
98 when it came to the molestation, "we will
99 probably never know what occurred."

100 But we did know because it had been
101 determined and there was no equivocation about
102 the fact that no abuse had taken place.
103 Justice Wilk was quite rough on me and never
104 approved of my relationship with Soon-Yi,
105 Mia's adopted daughter, who was then in her
106 early 20s. He thought of me as an older man
107 exploiting a much younger woman, which

108 outraged Mia as improper despite the fact she
109 had dated a much older Frank Sinatra when she
110 was 19. In fairness to Justice Wilk, the
111 public felt the same dismay over Soon-Yi and
112 myself, but despite what it looked like our
113 feelings were authentic and we've been happily
114 married for 16 years with two great kids, both
115 adopted. (Incidentally, coming on the heels of
116 the media circus and false accusations, Soon-
117 Yi and I were extra carefully scrutinized by
118 both the adoption agency and adoption courts,
119 and everyone blessed our adoptions.)

120 Mia took custody of the children and we went
121 our separate ways.

122 I was heartbroken. Moses was angry with me.
123 Ronan I didn't know well because Mia would
124 never let me get close to him from the moment
125 he was born and Dylan, whom I adored and was
126 very close to and about whom Mia called my
127 sister in a rage and said, "He took my
128 daughter, now I'll take his." I never saw her
129 again nor was I able to speak with her no
130 matter how hard I tried. I still loved her
131 deeply, and felt guilty that by falling in
132 love with Soon-Yi I had put her in the
133 position of being used as a pawn for revenge.
134 Soon-Yi and I made countless attempts to see
135 Dylan but Mia blocked them all, spitefully
136 knowing how much we both loved her but
137 totally indifferent to the pain and damage she
138 was causing the little girl merely to appease
139 her own vindictiveness.

140 Here I quote Moses Farrow, 14 at the time:
141 "My mother drummed it into me to hate my
142 father for tearing apart the family and
143 sexually molesting my sister." Moses is now 36
144 years old and a family therapist by profession.
145 "Of course Woody did not molest my sister," he

146 said. "She loved him and looked forward to
147 seeing him when he would visit. She never hid
148 from him until our mother succeeded in
149 creating the atmosphere of fear and hate
150 towards him." Dylan was 7, Ronan 4, and this
151 was, according to Moses, the steady narrative
152 year after year.

153 I pause here for a quick word on the Ronan
154 situation. Is he my son or, as Mia suggests,
155 Frank Sinatra's? Granted, he looks a lot like
156 Frank with the blue eyes and facial features,
157 but if so what does this say? That all during
158 the custody hearing Mia lied under oath and
159 falsely represented Ronan as our son? Even if
160 he is not Frank's, the possibility she raises
161 that he could be, indicates she was secretly
162 intimate with him during our years. Not to
163 mention all the money I paid for child
164 support. Was I supporting Frank's son? Again,
165 I want to call attention to the integrity and
166 honesty of a person who conducts her life like
167 that.

168 NOW it's 21 years later and Dylan has come
169 forward with the accusations that the Yale
170 experts investigated and found false. Plus a
171 few little added creative flourishes that seem
172 to have magically appeared during our 21-year
173 estrangement.

174 Not that I doubt Dylan hasn't come to believe
175 she's been molested, but if from the age of 7
176 a vulnerable child is taught by a strong
177 mother to hate her father because he is a
178 monster who abused her, is it so inconceivable
179 that after many years of this indoctrination
180 the image of me Mia wanted to establish had
181 taken root? Is it any wonder the experts at
182 Yale had picked up the maternal coaching
183 aspect 21 years ago? Even the venue where the

184 fabricated molestation was supposed to have
185 taken place was poorly chosen but interesting.
186 Mia chose the attic of her country house, a
187 place she should have realized I'd never go to
188 because it is a tiny, cramped, enclosed spot
189 where one can hardly stand up and I'm a major
190 claustrophobe. The one or two times she asked
191 me to come in there to look at something, I
192 did, but quickly had to run out. Undoubtedly
193 the attic idea came to her from the Dory
194 Previn song, "With My Daddy in the Attic." It
195 was on the same record as the song Dory Previn
196 had written about Mia's betraying their
197 friendship by insidiously stealing her husband,
198 André, "Beware of Young Girls." One must ask,
199 did Dylan even write the letter or was it at
200 least guided by her mother? Does the letter
201 really benefit Dylan or does it simply advance
202 her mother's shabby agenda? That is to hurt me
203 with a smear. There is even a lame attempt to
204 do professional damage by trying to involve
205 movie stars, which smells a lot more like Mia
206 than Dylan.

207 After all, if speaking out was really a
208 necessity for Dylan, she had already spoken
209 out months earlier in Vanity Fair. Here I
210 quote Moses Farrow again: "Knowing that my
211 mother often used us as pawns, I cannot trust
212 anything that is said or written from anyone
213 in the family." Finally, does Mia herself
214 really even believe I molested her daughter?
215 Common sense must ask: Would a mother who
216 thought her 7-year-old daughter was sexually
217 abused by a molester (a pretty horrific crime),
218 give consent for a film clip of her to be used
219 to honor the molester at the Golden Globes?

220 Of course, I did not molest Dylan. I loved
221 her and hope one day she will grasp how she
222 has been cheated out of having a loving father

223   and exploited by a mother more interested in
224   her own festering anger than her daughter's
225   well-being. Being taught to hate your father
226   and made to believe he molested you has
227   already taken a psychological toll on this
228   lovely young woman, and Soon-Yi and I are both
229   hoping that one day she will understand who
230   has really made her a victim and reconnect
231   with us, as Moses has, in a loving, productive
232   way. No one wants to discourage abuse victims
233   from speaking out, but one must bear in mind
234   that sometimes there are people who are
235   falsely accused and that is also a terribly
236   destructive thing. (This piece will be my
237   final word on this entire matter and no one
238   will be responding on my behalf to any further
239   comments on it by any party. Enough people
240   have been hurt.

Legend for the highlights in my analysis of Woody Allen's letter:

Denial

Pronouns and substitutes

Active-voice-past-tense

Active-voice-past-perfect-tense

Interesting words or phrases

Sentences with "had"

1   TWENTY-ONE years ago, when I first heard Mia

2   Farrow had accused me of child molestation, I

3   found the idea so ludicrous I didn't give it

4   a second thought. We were involved in a

5   terribly acrimonious breakup, with great

6   enmity between us and a custody battle slowly

7   gathering energy. The self-serving

8   transparency of her malevolence seemed so

9   obvious I didn't even hire a lawyer to defend

10 myself. It was my show business attorney who

11 told me she was bringing the accusation to

12 the police and I would need a criminal lawyer.

13 I naïvely thought the accusation would be

14 dismissed out of hand because of course, I

15 hadn't molested Dylan and any rational person

16 would see the ploy for what it was. Common

17 sense would prevail. After all, I was a 56-

18 year-old man who had never before (or after)

19 been accused of child molestation. I had been

20 going out with Mia for 12 years and never in

21 that time did she ever suggest to me anything

22 resembling misconduct. Now, suddenly, when I

23 had driven up to her house in Connecticut one

24 afternoon to visit the kids for a few hours,

25 when I would be on my raging adversary's home
26 turf, with half a dozen people present, when I
27 was in the blissful early stages of a happy
28 new relationship with the woman I'd go on to

29 marry — that I would pick this moment in time
30 to embark on a career as a child molester
31 should seem to the most skeptical mind highly
32 unlikely. The sheer illogic of such a crazy
33 scenario seemed to me dispositive.

34 Notwithstanding, Mia insisted that I had
35 abused Dylan and took her immediately to a
36 doctor to be examined. Dylan told the doctor
37 she had not been molested. Mia then took
38 Dylan out for ice cream, and when she came
39 back with her the child had changed her story.
40 The police began their investigation; a
41 possible indictment hung in the balance. I
42 very willingly took a lie-detector test and
43 of course passed because I had nothing to hide.
44 I asked Mia to take one and she wouldn't.
45 Last week a woman named Stacey Nelkin, whom I
46 had dated many years ago, came forward to the
47 press to tell them that when Mia and I first
48 had our custody battle 21 years ago, Mia had

49 wanted her to testify that she had been
50 underage when I was dating her, despite the
51 fact this was untrue. Stacey refused. I
52 include this anecdote so we all know what kind
53 of character we are dealing with here. One can
54 imagine in learning this why she wouldn't take
55 a lie-detector test.
56 Meanwhile the Connecticut police turned for
57 help to a special investigative unit they
58 relied on in such cases, the Child Sexual
59 Abuse Clinic of the Yale-New Haven Hospital.
60 This group of impartial, experienced men and
61 women whom the district attorney looked to for
62 guidance as to whether to prosecute, spent
63 months doing a meticulous investigation,
64 interviewing everyone concerned, and checking
65 every piece of evidence. Finally they wrote
66 their conclusion which I quote here: "It is
67 our expert opinion that Dylan was not sexually
68 abused by Mr. Allen. Further, we believe that
69 Dylan's statements on videotape and her
70 statements to us during our evaluation do not
71 refer to actual events that occurred to her on
72 August 4th, 1992... In developing our opinion
73 we considered three hypotheses to explain
74 Dylan's statements. First, that Dylan's
75 statements were true and that Mr. Allen had
76 sexually abused her; second, that Dylan's

78   an emotionally vulnerable child who was caught
79   up in a disturbed family and who was
80   responding to the stresses in the family; and
81   third, that Dylan was coached or influenced by
82   her mother, Ms. Farrow. While we can conclude
83   that Dylan was not sexually abused, we can not
84   be definite about whether the second
85   formulation by itself or the third formulation
86   by itself is true. We believe that it is more
87   likely that a combination of these two
88   formulations best explains Dylan's allegations
89   of sexual abuse."

90   Could it be any clearer? Mr. Allen did not
91   abuse Dylan; most likely a vulnerable,
92   stressed-out 7-year-old was coached by Mia
93   Farrow. This conclusion disappointed a number
94   of people. The district attorney was champing
95   at the bit to prosecute a celebrity case, and
96   Justice Elliott Wilk, the custody judge,
97   wrote a very irresponsible opinion saying
98   when it came to the molestation, "we will
99   probably never know what occurred."

100   But we did know because it had been
101   determined and there was no equivocation about
102   the fact that no abuse had taken place.

103 Justice Wilk was quite rough on me and never

104 approved of my relationship with Soon-Yi,

105 Mia's adopted daughter, who was then in her

106 early 20s. He thought of me as an older man

107 exploiting a much younger woman, which

108 outraged Mia as improper despite the fact she

109 had dated a much older Frank Sinatra when she

110 was 19. In fairness to Justice Wilk, the

111 public felt the same dismay over Soon-Yi and

112 myself, but despite what it looked like our

113 feelings were authentic and we've been happily

114 married for 16 years with two great kids, both

115 adopted. (Incidentally, coming on the heels of

116 the media circus and false accusations, Soon-

117 Yi and I were extra carefully scrutinized by

118 both the adoption agency and adoption courts,

119 and everyone blessed our adoptions.)

120 Mia took custody of the children and we went

121 our separate ways.

122 I was heartbroken. Moses was angry with me.

123 Ronan I didn't know well because Mia would

124 never let me get close to him from the moment

125 he was born and Dylan, whom I adored and was

126 very close to and about whom Mia called my

127 sister in a rage and said, "He took my

128 daughter, now I'll take his." I never saw her
129 again nor was I able to speak with her no
130 matter how hard I tried. I still loved her
131 deeply, and felt guilty that by falling in
132 love with Soon-Yi I had put her in the
133 position of being used as a pawn for revenge.
134 Soon-Yi and I made countless attempts to see
135 Dylan but Mia blocked them all, spitefully
136 knowing how much we both loved her but
137 totally indifferent to the pain and damage she
138 was causing the little girl merely to appease
139 her own vindictiveness.

140 Here I quote Moses Farrow, 14 at the time:
141 "My mother drummed it into me to hate my
142 father for tearing apart the family and
143 sexually molesting my sister." Moses is now 36
144 years old and a family therapist by profession.
145 "Of course Woody did not molest my sister," he
146 said. "She loved him and looked forward to
147 seeing him when he would visit. She never hid
148 from him until our mother succeeded in
149 creating the atmosphere of fear and hate
150 towards him." Dylan was 7, Ronan 4, and this
151 was, according to Moses, the steady narrative
152 year after year.

153   I pause here for a quick word on the Ronan

154   situation. Is he my son or, as Mia suggests,

155   Frank Sinatra's? Granted, he looks a lot like

156   Frank with the blue eyes and facial features,

157   but if so what does this say? That all during

158   the custody hearing Mia lied under oath and

159   falsely represented Ronan as our son? Even if

160   he is not Frank's, the possibility she raises

161   that he could be, indicates she was secretly

162   intimate with him during our years. Not to

163   mention all the money I paid for child

164   support. Was I supporting Frank's son? Again,

165   I want to call attention to the integrity and

166   honesty of a person who conducts her life like

167   that.

168   NOW it's 21 years later and Dylan has come

169   forward with the accusations that the Yale

170   experts investigated and found false. Plus a

171   few little added creative flourishes that seem

172   to have magically appeared during our 21-year

173   estrangement.

174   Not that I doubt Dylan hasn't come to believe

175   she's been molested, but if from the age of 7

176   a vulnerable child is taught by a strong

177   mother to hate her father because he is a

178 monster who abused her, is it so inconceivable
179 that after many years of this indoctrination
180 the image of me Mia wanted to establish had
181 taken root? Is it any wonder the experts at
182 Yale had picked up the maternal coaching
183 aspect 21 years ago? Even the venue where the
184 fabricated molestation was supposed to have
185 taken place was poorly chosen but interesting.
186 Mia chose the attic of her country house, a
187 place she should have realized I'd never go to
188 because it is a tiny, cramped, enclosed spot
189 where one can hardly stand up and I'm a major
190 claustrophobe. The one or two times she asked
191 me to come in there to look at something, I
192 did, but quickly had to run out. Undoubtedly
193 the attic idea came to her from the Dory
194 Previn song, "With My Daddy in the Attic." It
195 was on the same record as the song Dory Previn
196 had written about Mia's betraying their
197 friendship by insidiously stealing her husband,
198 André, "Beware of Young Girls." One must ask,
199 did Dylan even write the letter or was it at
200 least guided by her mother? Does the letter
201 really benefit Dylan or does it simply advance
202 her mother's shabby agenda? That is to hurt me
203 with a smear. There is even a lame attempt to

204 do professional damage by trying to involve

205 movie stars, which smells a lot more like Mia

206 than Dylan.

207 After all, if speaking out was really a

208 necessity for Dylan, she had already spoken

209 out months earlier in Vanity Fair. Here I

210 quote Moses Farrow again: "Knowing that my

211 mother often used us as pawns, I cannot trust

212 anything that is said or written from anyone

213 in the family." Finally, does Mia herself

214 really even believe I molested her daughter?

215 Common sense must ask: Would a mother who

216 thought her 7-year-old daughter was sexually

217 abused by a molester (a pretty horrific crime),

218 give consent for a film clip of her to be used

219 to honor the molester at the Golden Globes?

220 Of course, I did not molest Dylan. I loved

221 her and hope one day she will grasp how she

222 has been cheated out of having a loving father

223 and exploited by a mother more interested in

224 her own festering anger than her daughter's

225 well-being. Being taught to hate your father

226 and made to believe he molested you has

227 already taken a psychological toll on this

228 lovely young woman, and Soon-Yi and I are both

229 hoping that one day she will understand who

228 lovely young woman, and Soon-Yi and I are both
229 hoping that one day she will understand who
230 has really made her a victim and reconnect
231 with us, as Moses has, in a loving, productive
232 way. No one wants to discourage abuse victims
233 from speaking out, but one must bear in mind
234 that sometimes there are people who are
235 falsely accused and that is also a terribly
236 destructive thing. (This piece will be my
237 final word on this entire matter and no one
238 will be responding on my behalf to any further
239 comments on it by any party. Enough people
240 have been hurt.

Legend for the highlights in my analysis of Woody Allen's letter:

Denial

Pronouns and substitutes

Active-voice-past-tense

Active-voice-past-perfect-tense

Interesting words or phrases

Sentences with "had"

Woody Allen alternates between the active-voice-past-perfect-tense and the active-voice-past-tense. He uses the past perfect verb "had," often and in doing so, creates the past perfect tense, which makes for a complex statement. He can use the past-tense-active-voice as well, and switches in and out of those voices and tenses. That may be his typical writing style. In any case, he shows he can write in the active-voice-past-tense so the changes between the two are noteworthy and affords some interesting analysis. The active-voice-past-tense is much easier to interpret; whereas the active-voice-past-perfect-tense is much more difficult to construct and much more difficult to interpret. If we go back to the O.J. Simpson analysis, (13A, page 101), an innocent person wants to quickly declare innocence — and will do so with simple, direct, and precise denials which help prove their innocence. Woody Allen's statement isn't simple, direct, or precise — which makes this denial suspect at the onset.

There are two denials in the statement, the first one (line 13) in the active-voice-past-perfect-tense ("I naïvely thought the accusation would be dismissed out of hand because of course, I hadn't molested Dylan and any rational person would see the ploy for what it was.") and the last one (line 220) in the active-voice-past-tense voice ("Of course, I did not molest Dylan.").

Once again, we look for simplicity, directness, and precision in denials. Anything else is suspicious. If the denial has an introduction, a qualifier, a wiggle word, or anything that detracts from simplicity, directness, and precision — it is suspect. The denial, "I didn't do it," when everyone knows what "it" is, and there is no "wiggle" in "it," is the best denial. It has simplicity, directness, and precision. It also has the contraction, "didn't," which connotes a lower level of stress — and we all know that someone telling the truth is under less stress. So, contractions are a plus — but we must be careful, and calibrate our analysis to the individual. If the individual always uses a contraction, the use of a contraction is less indicative of less stress. Woody Allen uses a contraction 14 times in his statement. We need to look at where those are and whether they are used in critical areas, where stress might be elevated.

Woody Allen's first denial appears at line 13: "I naïvely thought the accusation would be dismissed out of hand because of course, I hadn't molested Dylan and any rational person would see the ploy for what it was." The phrase, "I hadn't molested Dylan," is notable. Question: Is that a simple, direct, and precise denial?

This first denial does contain a contraction, ". . . because, of course, I hadn't molested Dylan. . . ." That is a plus, but it is in the past-perfect-tense, which is less than desirable.

Dylan's accusation is on line 8 in her statement: "he sexually assaulted me." She used the word "sexual" 4 additional times in her statement. Nowhere in her statement does she use the word, "molest," or any derivation of that word. So, the precision part of Mr. Allen's denial is suspect. Dylan didn't accuse him of "molesting" her, she accused him of "sexually assaulting" her, a much more painful, descriptive, and specific action. The word, "molest," may include "sexual assault," but it also includes "harass," "pester," and other actions that are significantly less repulsive than "sexual assault." So, by saying, "I hadn't molested," Mr. Allen chose to soften and minimize the accusation.

No one can reliably characterize Woody Allen's above denial as simple or direct. I would expect something like, "I didn't sexually assault my daughter, Dylan." That's a simple and direct denial. There is little wiggle room in those words. There is wiggle in his denial. We know he's capable of stating things simply as he did in line 2, "I found the idea so ludicrous I didn't give it a second thought." Or, line 37, "Mia then took Dylan out for ice cream, and when she came back with her the child had changed her story." Or line 44, "I asked Mia to take one and she wouldn't." So, he shows that he can write simply and directly. So, he could have stated, "I didn't sexually assault my daughter, Dylan," but he chose not to.

Let's look at the structure of the denial. "I naïvely thought the accusation would be dismissed out of hand because of course, I hadn't molested Dylan and any rational person would see the ploy for what it was." First of all, the reference to "the accusation" is less precise than "my daughter's accusation" or "her accusation." He also introduces the denial with, "I naively thought," which reveals his egocentrism. One would expect a father who hears his daughter is accusing him of sexual assault would first think of his daughter. If not a true allegation, his response wouldn't be a calculation as in, "I naively thought," or "see the ploy for what it was;" rather, it would be "how could that be?" or, "what is happening to my daughter to cause her to accuse me?"

It's also very interesting that he never refers to Dylan as his daughter. There are no, "my daughter's, in his statement — and that is telling. That depersonalization is consistent with the wording in his denial in that he always refers to her as "Dylan," and he minimizes and softens the accusation by referring to it as a molestation ("I hadn't molested Dylan") instead of using the words "sexually assault," which is the precise wording in the accusation. We often see a depersonalization in abuser's recounting of the violent event. As in the JonBenét Ramsay case, the parents never referred to their deceased daughter as "my daughter." They always called her JonBenét. A name carries much less emotion than a "my daughter." There are other JonBenét's. There is only one, "my daughter." Likewise, there are many Dylans.

He uses, "of course," in lines 14, 43, and 220. All relate to the "molestation," and his denial. Line 14: "I naïvely thought the accusation would be dismissed out of hand because <u>of course</u>, I hadn't molested Dylan and any rational person would see the ploy for what it was." Line 43: "I very willingly took a lie-detector test and <u>of course</u> passed because I had nothing to hide." And Line 220: "<u>Of course</u>, I did not molest Dylan." It's almost as if Woody Allen is responding to a voice or carrying on a conversation. He is, of course, being asked the question from Dylan's accusation: "Did you sexually assault your daughter, Dylan?" To which he responds, "Of course, I did not <u>molest</u> Dylan." Does this ("of course") affect the validity of his denial? Yes.

Repetitive denial patterns diminish the validity of all the denials. It reveals a lack of spontaneity, genuineness, a lack of thought, and a lack of meaningfulness. The "of course," also sets up an expectation when the truth requires no introduction or expectation. The truth stands on its own, by itself. Denials with introductions are suspicious.

The vast majority of this statement refers to Mia and "the ploy," as opposed to the sexual assault accusation. The entire opening paragraph relates to Mia's alleged scheme against him. I would expect a denial to devote much greater time to the accusation.

Again, his initial response is all about him, with no apparent concern for his daughter. That alone doesn't tell us that he is guilty, but it does provide us with further insight into this attempt at a denial. He is apparently unable to provide a simple, direct, precise, and clear denial. He devotes almost his entire denial letter to Mia and her "ploy." He doesn't offer a denial until the second paragraph, and that is yet another notable event. Mia's name appears 21 times in his statement. Dylan's name appears 23 times, and never is she identified as "my daughter." In line

220, he states, "I loved her," which is past tense and reveals his current feelings toward his daughter, whom he calls a "victim."

Woody Allen's statement is not a good denial, is self-serving, and reflects a man who continues to proclaim his innocence without giving us sufficient reason to believe him. A poor denial is evidence the allegations are true. Dylan's account still stands as a monument to truth and veracity.